THE FORM OF MUSIC

D0928423

Wᴉʟʟɪᴀᴍ Cᴏʟᴇ

The Form of Music

The Associated Board of
the Royal Schools of Music

The Associated Board of the Royal Schools of Music (Publishing) Ltd
24 Portland Place, London W1B 1LU, United Kingdom

First edition published 1969
Second edition published 1970; reprinted 1973, 1976, 1979, 1982
Second edition reissued in paperback 1997, reprinted 1999, 2001, 2003, 2004,
2005, 2007, 2009

© 1969 and 1997 by The Associated Board of the Royal Schools of Music

paperback ISBN 1 86096 027 8

All rights reserved. No part of this publication may be reproduced, stored
in a retrieval system, or transmitted in any form or by any means, electronic,
mechanical, photocopying, recording, or otherwise, without the prior
permission of the copyright owner.

Some of the definitions in the glossary are taken from the author's *Rudiments of
Music: Music Primer No. 130* by kind permission of Novello & Co. Ltd.

Printed in Great Britain by Caligraving Limited, Thetford, Norfolk

ACKNOWLEDGEMENTS

I am indebted to Mr. Walter Emery, who made valuable sugges-
tions after reading the first draft, and to Dr. Herbert Howells
and Mr. Patrick Savill, members of the Associated Board, who
read and suggested improvements in the final draft. I must
thank Mrs. Favell and Miss Kentish who typed my manuscript,
and Mr. Douglas J. Reeves, Publishing Manager of the Associated
Board, who overcame the many problems that arose in seeing
the book through the press.

WILLIAM COLE

CONTENTS

CHAPTER ONE

Introduction

What is Musical Form? Briefly it is the structural plan of a musical composition. Many of the works written in the last three centuries will fit more or less into stock designs. They are fairly easy to recognise and their recognition is helpful as a starting point to a further study of the music.

How does form come to be a musical attribute? One of the definitions in the *Oxford English Dictionary* is 'visible aspect', another 'the arrangement of the parts'. This is easy to see in architecture, painting or sculpture. A building occupies a certain number of cubic feet and its visible aspect is there to be studied and measured at any time. If the arrangement of the parts is well-balanced and unified the building has a satisfactory form. Of course, it is not as simple as that; for instance, the architect tries to ensure that his building has a satisfactory aspect from a variety of viewpoints, but the argument is broadly true. A painting occupies a certain area of canvas and the arrangement of its parts can always be seen. When one looks at a building or a painting one can take it in at a single glance. This is the 'coup d'oeil'; the first impression that can be expanded by more leisurely study.

Music occupies a certain length of time, and the only physical means of measuring it is by minutes and seconds. It has no 'visible aspect' and any form it might have can be recognised only through the ear. What will give a series of aural impressions lasting, say, three minutes, design? First, it is necessary to analyse the process of listening. Music is a succession of sounds, simple or complex. The ear hears the first sound and links it to the second. The first is still in the memory as the second is followed by the third. This process continues like a cinematograph of sound and there is an illusion of onward movement. Memory enables the sounds to be compared, and it is possible for most people to remember a series of sounds that form a pattern lasting a few seconds. If one is accustomed to listening one often knows what to expect; and while the ear is listening to the present the mind is anticipating the future and remembering the past. It is an existence on three planes, the mind roaming backwards and forwards whilst the physical ear is concerned only with the present.

Musical memory varies with the individual. It is said that Mozart at the age of 14 after hearing Allegri's *Miserere* in the Sistine Chapel at the Vatican wrote the whole work out from memory after the service. The work is in four and five parts with a final nine-part chorus. This showed a superhuman memory, but many lesser folk can remember quite long stretches of music. One cannot take in a piece of music with a 'coup d'oeil' as in the plastic arts. The musical equivalent would be the first pattern of sound which might be long enough to be called a phrase. There is much more to be heard after the first phrase. The second phrase may repeat what has gone before, or it may develop the first, or it may contrast. If it repeats it must eventually develop or contrast because a satisfactory form cannot be made by repeating an opening many times. Very often a repetition of the opening is made after a period of contrast. It is the design made by repetition, development and contrast that determines the form of the music. At a first hearing it is often difficult to remember the various phrases but repetitions jog the memory. Also, a knowledge of musical notation enables one to grasp the sounds more quickly. The eye looking at a score assists the ear by following the pattern of the notes; but the form of the music must be intelligible through the ear. The story of the evolution of music is to some extent that of composers trying to give their works length. There is a tremendous difference in this respect even between Haydn's First Symphony and Beethoven's Ninth.

This book sets out to study the forms in common use during the last 300 years. It is presumed that the reader is sufficiently interested to have his own copies of the pianoforte sonatas of Haydn,* Mozart and Beethoven and the two books of the '48',

* The numbering of the Haydn Sonatas used in this book is that of the Hoboken Catalogue.

and to have a fair knowledge of these works. If not, he is advised to buy them and hear or play them and to spend his time absorbing music itself rather than reading books about the subject. He should have access to the *Historical Anthology of Music** by Davison and Apel which is necessary for the chapters on the early sonata and the early contrapuntal forms.

The quickest way to find information about a form is to consult the glossary-index. Either it will be described there, or the page given where it will be found.

---

* In two volumes published by Oxford University Press. In the text abbreviated to HAM, followed by the number of the example.

CHAPTER TWO

Phrase and Cadence

The form of a piece may be found by examination of its constituent parts. The smallest musical unit is called a *Figure* and is a group of notes in a time-pattern. To produce a pattern there must be at least one accent, but there may be two or more. The obvious place to find a figure is at the start of a composition, as in Exs. 1–4. The figure is under a square bracket.

The composer may add to the opening figure in various ways. Four common ones are shown below:

Ex.1   Beethoven, Sonata in E flat major, Op. 31, No. 3
                                    2nd movement, bars 1–5

The figure lasts for a bar and is repeated a 3rd higher, a second figure is introduced in bar 3.

Ex.2   Mozart, Sonata in C minor, (K.457)
                                    bars 1–5

The figure (Ex. 2) lasts for 1½ bars, and a contrasted figure at the third beat of bar 2 acts as a foil to the first.

Ex.3

Beethoven, Violin Concerto in D major, Op. 61
2nd movement, bars 1–5

The opening figure is repeated exactly, and its opening rhythm links it on to a new figure at bar 3.

Ex.4

Wagner, 'Flying Dutchman' Overture
bars 65–69

The opening smooth figure which goes to the first two beats of bar 2 is followed by one that leaps a 4th and a 6th in bar 2. The arpeggio figure in bars 3–4 uses notes of the tonic chord rising from a′ in bar 3 to c″, a tenth above, in bar 4.

Each of the above extensions of a figure makes a musical *phrase*, and that word is used to describe the music in bars 1–4 of each example. It will be noticed that whereas Exs. 1, 2 and 4 begin on the first beat of a bar, Ex. 3 begins on the last beat. They may all be described as 4-bar phrases, because phrases are counted according to the number of accents (i.e. first beats of the bar) they contain. The music at the end of the bar leads towards the accent, and we begin numbering the bars, in any piece of music, from the first accent as shown in Ex. 3. A beginning before a main accent is called an anacrusis.

The curved lines in these examples are called phrase marks, but the name is often misleading. The purpose of the curved lines is to indicate that the notes under it should be played legato. Sometimes the phrase marks and the division of the piece into phrases coincide. In analysing a piece, one should not be misled by the phrase marks. The curved line has other uses in instrumental music. In string music it shows the number of notes to be played with one stroke of the bow and in wind music the number of notes to be taken in one breath.

It would be absurd to think of a composer writing a short figure and wondering how he would follow it. He would normally think of the whole of the opening phrase, if not more; for the phrase is only part of a larger section and like the figure needs more to follow it.

The *Oxford English Dictionary* describes a phrase as 'a short and more-or-less independent passage forming part of a longer passage or of a whole piece'. This implies that it has a definite ending, yet requires something else to follow it. Exs. 1–4 show this. Each requires another one or more phrases to follow before any sense of completion is felt. Art-forms which take place in time, such as poetry or music, require a certain length to make their effect. The ear knows that something else must follow after the opening phrase, and expects an answering phrase. When Shakespeare says:

'Hark, hark! the lark at heaven's gate sings'
there is a definite picture created in the mind, but it would be a disappointment if it ended there.

Two phrases in succession, opening and answering, make a musical *Sentence* or *Period*. A sentence, however, may be of three or four phrases, since the composer may not give a direct answering phrase immediately but may let the second phrase go further afield. Simple structures such as short songs or hymn tunes may consist of only one sentence; but the sentence will normally require more to follow it.

The reader must be warned against trying to see too close an analogy between grammatical and musical analysis. Every noun has a meaning, but a single musical sound merely establishes a pitch. It is not until sounds are associated together in a rhythmic scheme that music makes sense. A well-known sentence in the New Testament creates its effect by using two words, but a musical sentence requires length to do this. A phrase in English is 'a small group of words usually without predicate' (O.E.D.), but in music this would almost be equivalent to the figure. A musical phrase is more important and longer.

All the phrases in Exs. 1–4 were four bars in length. How does one know when a phrase ends? There is no easy answer; but at intervals the music seems to ebb a little and gather itself together for a fresh advance. These moments of repose are the phrase endings known as cadence points.

Phrase and cadence point had their origin in singing. It is generally accepted that man's first musical attempts were in song and that singing began as speech on a higher plane. In speaking and singing there must be pauses for breath. These pauses are the origin of the cadence. With each breath the voice would gradually rise in intensity and interest and at the end it would fall away.

The early music for instruments was not much different from that for voices, but as soon as composers realised the capabilities of instruments, an instrumental style evolved. Vocal music and instrumental music existed side by side for many centuries and still do so. Although they have trod separate paths, the legacy of phrasing is still inherent in instrumental music.

In vocal music the phrase-lengths and cadences are suited to verbal ends. In instrumental music it is not always so easy to find the cadences. Of the two original features, the pause for breath and the fall in the voice, only the first is usually found. It is shown either by a long note, a rest or a slight break between two sounds. The fall in the voice was never so important as the pause for breath, and there are many examples of early melodies with rising endings. With the development of harmony certain chords came to be associated with the cadence points. However, every long note, rest or break does not necessarily make a cadence point, and certain harmonies which form cadences do not make a cadence every time they are heard. This perhaps makes the question appear complicated, but the movement of the phrase to its cadence is much easier heard than explained in words.

There is much repetition in music and one can tell the length of a phrase by observing the repeat of an opening pattern (but see 'Overlapping of phrases', page 10, and Ex. 9). The harmonies used at cadences became stereotyped and the four common forms are the perfect, plagal, imperfect and interrupted. The reader should have a knowledge of these chords and also of chord progression in general to help in deciding phrase-endings.

Ex. 1 ends with an imperfect cadence in bar 4 which leads the way to a repetition of the opening figure at bar 5. The figure is easily remembered because of its *sf* on an unaccented part of the bar.

In Ex. 2, bar 5 imitates bar 1 on the dominant chord. There is an imperfect cadence (first inversion of tonic to the 2nd inversion of the dominant 9th) and a crotchet rest at bar 4.

In Ex. 3, bar 4, the phrase ends with a long note on an imperfect cadence in B minor (although a perfect cadence in that key is never reached). Bars 3 and 4 balance 1 and 2. The last beat of bar 4 repeats the opening rhythmic figure and so starts a new phrase.

Ex. 4 ends with an imperfect cadence with a ritardando to underline it. (The c″ of the melody really occupies the whole bar, the d″ being a decoration.) A rest at the end of bar 4 leads to a repetition of the melody an octave higher.

In Ex. 2 the melody falls at the cadence. Although there are rises in Exs. 1, 3 and 4, the general direction of the movement from the middle of each of the phrases is downwards. In Ex. 4 there is a definite rise up to c″. These examples, taken at random, show the distance instrumental music has travelled from the original meaning of the word cadence.

All these phrases are four bars long and that is the common length. At a quick tempo the phrase may be lengthened to eight bars or at a slower tempo shortened to two bars. Our first

introduction to music will probably have been in the four-bar
phrases of nursery rhymes, simple songs or hymn tunes. The
four-bar phrase becomes such a part of our musical existence
that any other length seems odd. The training of a music student
often begins by making him write phrases of varying length.
Composers try to avoid the monotonous effect of a continuous
string of four-bar phrases and purposely use other phrase lengths.
This can be done in three ways: (a) By establishing an opening
phrase of any length other than four bars; (b) By beginning a
second phrase with the last note of the first, thus making what is
called an overlapping phrase; (c) By answering a four-bar phrase
with one of different length. Examples of each of these methods
are shown below:

(a) *Opening phrases of different lengths*

An opening phrase of three bars is followed by one of two bars.
Then the next three-bar phrase is followed by a four-bar phrase
(not shown in the example). Then follows an 8-bar sentence
followed by one of nine bars. Purcell varies his phrase-lenghs and
is interesting to study for this alone, apart from his greatness as a
composer.

An opening phrase of three bars followed by one of five bars.

Ex.7
Brahms, 'St. Anthony' Variations, Op. 56a
bars 1–6

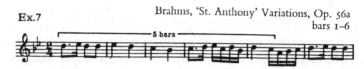

An opening phrase of five bars which is answered by one of five bars (not shown).

Ex.8
Hymn Tune, 'Praise to the Lord'
(Lobe den Herren)

An opening phrase of six bars repeated, followed by a five and a four.

(b) *Overlapping of phrases*

So far the examples have been of a melody alone or a melody with accompaniment. But music often has two melodies sounding at the same time and they need not be identical in phrase length. Very often they will overlap and thus encourage the onward movement. Overlapping is common in music for two instruments or in a song and accompaniment.

Ex. 9 shows overlapping melodies.

Ex.9
Beethoven, Sonata in C minor (*Pathétique*), Op. 13
2nd movement, bars 37–41 (melodies only shown)

Adagio cantabile

(c) *Answering a four-bar phrase by one of different length*

The answering phrase will be either expanded or contracted. The former is more common and the expansion can take place during the course of the phrase or at its cadence. The methods are:

(1) By repetition of some part of the phrase.

Ex.10

(Stölzel), 'Bist du bei mir'
from Little Notebook for Anna Magdalena Bach

The extra bar in the answering phrase is caused by the repetition of bar 5.

Ex.11
Allegretto

Haydn, Symphony, No. 88 in G major
Trio from 3rd movement, bars 1–10

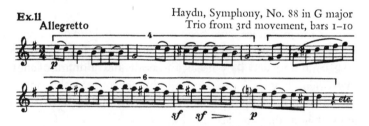

The extra two bars are caused by the repetition of bar 6, the second repetition being slightly varied.

(2) By expansion of part of the phrase and/or the addition of new material.

Ex.12 Con moto moderato

Brahms, Requiem, Op. 45
Soprano part, movement IV, bars 5–13

The extra bar in the answering phrase is caused by the lengthening of the g".

Haydn, Sonata No. 38 in E flat major
2nd movement, bars 1–9

Ex.13

The first phrase ends at bar 4 and the second phrase is expanded to 5 bars by sequence in bar 8 and addition of new material.

(3) The last note of the phrase may be held or the final chord repeated.

(C. P. E. Bach) March
from Little Notebook for Anna Magdalena Bach

Ex.14

Ex. 14 is a responsive phrase which has been lengthened from 4 bars to 5 by repetitions of the notes which make up the final chord.

(4) The cadence may be repeated one or more times.

The cadence (imperfect) is reached on the 1st beat of bar 16; it is then repeated seven times to the 1st beat of bar 21. But the phrase does not end here as the new descending figure is repeated and enlarged, the phrase coming to rest on the fourth quaver in bar 24.

(5) The cadence may be augmented.

Ex. 16 shows both repetition and augmentation.

(6) The cadence may be interrupted and the phrase extended.

The final phrase is extended by two bars because of the interrupted cadence.

(7) The shortening of a responsive phrase is not common. It is generally achieved through diminution of note values.

Ex. 18 shows a four-bar phrase answered by a three-bar phrase. In bar 7 the chords are compressed and a cadence is reached on the last beat of the bar.

CHAPTER THREE

Simple Binary and Ternary Forms

The first two words that a student learns in lessons on Form are binary and ternary. He also knows, or thinks he does, exactly what they mean. Binary is a piece that divides into two parts and ternary one that divides into three. It all seems very simple; and it would be if composers would write according to the book. Although there are many pieces that are binary or ternary there are also many that do not divide so definitely. In these cases the books on form disagree, some saying binary and some ternary; and, to make things more difficult, some writers have invented new methods of description. However, the words binary and ternary are still in common use, and must be explained. From an examination standpoint, the reasoning is more important than the label and for pieces that have elements of both binary and ternary either answer would be accepted if it were supported by evidence.

Simple Binary Form

At first this was used for short movements. It will be found in the seventeenth and eighteenth century suites, and is suited to the short dance movements which were in vogue then. Since about the middle of the eighteenth century composers have made little use of it, except for small piano pieces. Examples occur in Schumann's *Album for the Young* and Mendelssohn's *Songs without Words*. Many simple songs and hymn tunes are in binary form.

'The Holly and the Ivy'
(Gloucestershire Folk Song)

Ex.19

(*Reproduced by permission of Novello & Co. Ltd.*)

The four lines of the words are shown by the commas in the music, the main break coming at bar 4. The two parts are equal in length, and the note next in importance to the tonic—the dominant—ends the first section. In musical content, the two parts are different, the first showing a rise of a sixth in bars 1 and 3 and the second using quaver scale-passages, descending in bars 4–5 and ascending in bars 6–7. The drop of a fifth in bars 5–6, extending through to a sixth (b′–e′–d′), helps to preserve the unity of the song.

In many pieces of this type the first cadence is on the dominant, without modulation, but the effect is often made stronger by modulating as in Ex. 20.

Ex.20   Hymn Tune 'O God, our Help', *St. Anne* (Croft)

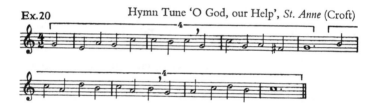

There is a definite modulation to the dominant at bar 4. The two sections are similar in rhythm and in their general type of movement. The rise of the fourth which appears three times in the first part is used once in the second.

In the eighteenth century suite the first part of a binary movement normally modulated to the dominant; or, if the movement were in the minor, to the relative major, or the dominant minor; or merely ended on the dominant chord, without modulating. There are exceptions. In the eight suites of Purcell there are two movements in which the tonic chord is used for the end of both parts. The same happens in the Menuet II of the French Suite in D minor by Bach. Occasionally the first section ends on a dominant chord and the second section begins in the tonic or reaches it in a bar or two. In general, however, it can be said that the progress of the first part is towards the dominant.

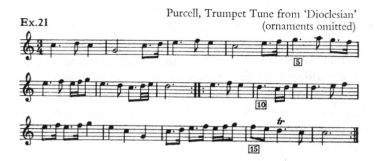

Ex.21

Purcell, Trumpet Tune from 'Dioclesian'
(ornaments omitted)

Ex. 21 shows a species of binary form in which each section is of the same length. There are eight bars in each part with the first ending on the chord of the dominant (there is no modulation). The dotted crotchet figure is the main feature of the first part; the second has heightened interest because of the dotted quavers in bars 12 and 14. Each part is repeated, making thirty-two bars in all.

Ex.22

Bach, Menuet from French Suite No. 6

The more common type of binary movement, eight bars answered by sixteen. The first part modulates to the dominant, and the second begins in the dominant and works back to the tonic. The return journey goes to C sharp minor at bar 12/13. At bar 17 there is a passing reference to the opening theme. This is not quite so marked when heard because the bass part is different from that used at the opening. The opening of the second section in B major (bars 9 and 10) is an exact transposition of the opening of the first section. In this movement the second section is longer than the first—eight bars are answered by sixteen. This became customary. Modulation to the dominant is easy, and quickly done, but in coming back to the tonic other keys are passed through, to give variety, and this takes more time.

In binary form there may be very little repetition (Ex. 22) or none at all (Ex. 21). It nevertheless gives an impression of coherence. This is partly because it represents at its best a development of one or two opening figures and partly because of its key scheme which is almost always symmetrical, the first part moving from tonic to dominant (or the relative key), and the second part returning.

Another feature which gives coherence is the similarity that often occurs between the last bars of the first part and those of the second part. Although this does not apply in Exs. 21 and 22 it will be found in Ex. 27. Bars 5 and 6 in the dominant correspond with bars 11 and 12 in the tonic.

Simple Ternary Form

In the three sections that make ternary form, the first and the third are similar. The third section may be shorter or longer than the first, it may be varied in detail or be an ornamental version, but the essential requirement is that the opening section shall be repeated in some recognizable way.

Ex. 23 is an illustration of a symmetrical piece in ternary form. The first section, a sad melody in D minor, has eight bars. The second section, a gay, quick dance in D major, also has eight bars (with the repeat). The third section uses the same melody as the first (except for one grace-note) but the melody is in a lower register for the first four bars and in octaves for the last four.

There are several other examples of ternary form in Schumann's *Album for the Young*, but the middle section is not always such a contrast. In a short piece, too much contrast destroys unity. Often the key remains the same and the theme of the second section is only slightly different from the first.

Ex.23
Plaintively

Schumann, Little Folksong, No. 9 from Album
for the Young, Op. 68

This simple ternary, A B A, is very rare in folk songs or national melodies for the simple reason that a three, or six-line stanza is a rarity.

Most examples of ternary form in folk songs or national songs divide the normal four lines of the verse as follows:

Line 1	Tune A
Line 2	Tune A
Line 3	Tune B
Line 4	Tune A

Well known examples (which are not quoted) are *The Ash Grove*, *The Minstrel Boy*, *The Vicar of Bray*, *The Tailor and the Mouse*. These are A A B A.

Now if we write AABA as ‖ : A : ‖ BA ‖ we have two equal divisions which Tovey says should logically be called binary. Which is more important, equality of length or repetition of theme? If we hold to the first, the above structure is binary; if to the second, it is ternary. Repetition always strikes the listener forcibly; he is much less likely to be conscious of the relative lengths of sections; and for this reason it is generally accepted that ternary is the correct label for this type of form.

Another deciding factor is that of key. The dependence of the second part on the first is marked in binary form because the first part usually ends in the dominant. In ternary form the first part usually ends in the tonic and can therefore stand by itself. This is so in *The Ash Grove* and the other songs mentioned above. Even here our demand for length is such that we feel something ought to follow on the first part; but that feeling becomes a necessity when the first section ends in the dominant, as it does in binary.

In the larger structures the difference between binary and ternary is generally clear; but in small pieces, which usually have little contrast of key or thematic material, the line of demarcation is not always clear. (Ex. 24)

In Ex. 24, the Minuet and Trio from Haydn's Quartet Op. 3, No. 6, both sections have a return to the main theme. In the Minuet, the return is at bar 17 and in the Trio at bar 33. The Minuet modulates to the dominant at the double bar, but the Trio does not. It could be argued therefore that the Minuet is in binary form and the Trio ternary. It seems absurd to describe procedures so similar with different names.* Binary and ternary are convenient enough labels for extended pieces, but are not always suitable for the smaller ones.

---

* Examination students imagine that there must be always a clear cut answer and that they will be penalised for the use of the wrong label. The examiner is more concerned with the reasoning than with the label and needs to know whether or not a candidate can recognise modulations and phrase-lengths. But if a student feels he must affix a label he could be guided by the amount of the opening which comes back at the end and how much from that point is in the tonic key.

Haydn, Quartet, Op. 3, No. 6
3rd movement

Ex. 24

Menuetto D.C.

CHAPTER FOUR

Ternary Form and its Simple Extensions— Rondo Form

Ternary Form in its simple plan of statement, digression, re-statement (ABA) has been used for many pieces both vocal and instrumental. Sometimes each of the three sections breaks down into a binary or ternary structure. Nineteenth-century composers often tried to avoid making a stop between the sections, merging A into B and B into A. To give a greater sense of finality a short coda (*q.v.*) may follow the third section. The first A may be preceded by an introduction.

One of the most usual methods of maintaining the interest is to vary the treatment of A on its return. This gives a sense of progression, since the return of A is more intense than its first appearance.

The various names given to the Ternary structure are:
(a) Aria Form or Song Form.
(b) Minuet and Trio Form.
(c) Episodical Form.

Aria Form

Many eighteenth-century arias are in this form. Well-known examples are 'Rejoice greatly' from Handel's *Messiah* and 'Break in Grief' from Bach's *St. Matthew Passion*. The three sections are often quite distinct. The middle section is generally in a related key and more lightly accompanied. At the return the singer was expected to add embellishments to the composer's written notes and to show his ability by a decoration of the cadence (the origin of the word 'cadenza'). Much of the decoration must have become stereotyped. After the first few performances of an aria, a singer would realise the most suitable variation and presumably would tend to keep to it at later performances. In most modern performances these variations are omitted and the authentic flavour is thereby lost, but perhaps the loss is all to the good. For the few singers who could bring this off and make it sound really effective there must have been many who were crashing bores.

Alessandro Scarlatti has been credited with the invention of this form, but perhaps it would be more true to say that he stabilised it by continual use. The usual form was:

A¹ { Instrumental introduction generally on the main vocal theme
Vocal solo beginning and ending in the tonic key
Instrumental closing section.

B   Vocal solo in a related key, usually with more modulation than A and often more lightly accompanied.

A²   As above, but often omitting the introduction.

In most instances, the repeat of A was not written out but was indicated by the words 'da capo' at the end of B. The instrumental opening was called a 'ritornello' or a 'symphony'. This is an early use of the latter word and merely implied something sounding on instruments as distinct from something sung. The word 'ritornello' means 'refrain'; originally it described the later appearance of the instrumental introduction, but eventually it described the opening instrumental section as well.

Minuet and Trio Form

In the classical symphony, the minuet and trio followed the slow movement. So common was this, and so invariable its form (minuet – trio – minuet) that the name is used to describe the structure. The musical material is usually simple, and the dance element tends to make the phrases clear-cut. This simplicity is emphasised because each section is complete in itself and shows either a simple binary or ternary shape. Ex. 24 is typical, the return to the opening being shown by the words *Menuetto D.C.* at the end of the trio. The convention is that the repeats of the menuetto are omitted when it is played for the second time. In Ex. 24 each section. minuet and trio is divided

into two parts, and the trio is in a related key. The structure is
easily grasped; the opening melody with its characteristic dance
rhythm can be quickly spotted at its reappearance. If one's ear
is poor and one's memory weak, listening to such movements
from the works of Haydn, Mozart and early Beethoven is
useful practice.

Episodical Form

An episode is a section of a piece that occurs only once (for
a different meaning of the word see Chapter 9, page 124).
Any piece in ternary form is therefore episodic, but the word
is usually restricted to a large-scale ternary form in which
the middle section is of a contrasted nature—more contrasted
than minuet and trio. Further, instead of the clear-cut divisions
of the minuet and trio, the sections are linked together, or there
is an imperceptible merging of one with the other. The whole
tends to be more subtle than its straightforward predecessor.
Examples may be found in eighteenth- and nineteenth-century
composers; see, for instance Mozart Sonata in C major (K.330),
Andante Cantabile; Beethoven Op. 31 No. 1 Adagio grazioso;
Chopin Fantasie-Impromptu in C sharp minor Op. 66; Brahms
Intermezzo, Op. 118 No. 2.

Extension of the Ternary Form

After ABA it is a simple extension to add another episode and
round the work off by repeating the main theme—ABACA.
The repetition of A binds the music together and the composer
would be careful to see that C was well contrasted to both
A and B. This structure is known under two names: (1) minuet
with two trios, (2) rondo (or old rondo). The latter is common,
but the former is not. However, Mozart, Beethoven, Schumann
and Brahms have composed minuets with two trios, one of the
best known being that of Mozart's Clarinet Quintet (K.581).
Mozart varies the instrumentation as well as the mode of the two
trios, but the drawback to the form is that the triple appearance
of the minuet makes for monotony. The same happened in early

rondos, but in the later ones of Haydn, Mozart and Beethoven the theme is varied at its repeat, and because of the larger scale of the composition the episodes gain in importance.

Ex. 25 Rameau, Les Tendres Plaintes, Rondeau

Ex. 25 is an early 'rondeau' by Rameau entitled *Les tendres plaintes*. Its main theme is in D minor and shows the sensitivity and clarity typical of a French composer, and well illustrates its title. The complete piece consists of 80 bars, made up of five sections (ABACA) each of 16 bars. The key scheme is equally simple, B being in A minor and C in F major. Only the melody is quoted and the repeats of A (which are identical) are abbreviated. Notice that A itself is in simple binary form, and although B and C are different they both begin with the simple rhythm that characterises A.

Interesting examples in which the key of the main theme is varied are to be found in the works of C. P. E. Bach. In Rondo I of the Fourth collection of Sonatas, Free Fantasias and Rondos for Connoisseurs and Music Lovers, the scheme is as follows:

A.   Main theme in A major (8 bars—a 4-bar theme repeated).
B.   New theme modulation to E major (8 bars).
A.   E major (9 bars).
C.   New theme in A minor (4 bars).
A.   C major (7 bars).
D.   Cadenza (D minor, E minor, G major).
A.   G major (4 bars).
E.   Opening figure of A extended, modulating to B minor.
A.   B minor (4 bars).
F.   Cadenza (8 bars) modulating to A major.
A.   A major (original key 8 bars).
G.   Cadenza.
A.   B flat major (4 bars).
H.   Cadenza (12 bars).
A.   A major (9 bars).

The scheme looks formidable and unmusical; but in fact there is a great deal of variety in the presentation of the main theme, and the whole is effective. The episodes are not all distinct thematically and some carry on naturally from the theme. The main theme is quoted in Ex. 26.

C. P. E. Bach, Rondo, No. 1 from the fourth collection of Sonatas, Free Fantasias and Rondos for Connoisseurs and Music Lovers

Ex.26

Andantino

bars 1–4

A Rondeau by D'Anglebert* which extends to ABACADAFA is another example of the longer form. Section A is the same at each appearance, and it need hardly be said that one wonders when the end will come.

* Early Keyboard Music Vol. I. G. Schirmer, New York.

Bach occasionally used the form, using the French heading Rondeau in Partita No. 2 and in the Orchestral Suite in B minor. Later composers gave more variety to the Rondo. The following should be studied; Haydn, Last movement of Piano Trio in G; Mozart, Rondo in A minor (K.511) and the last movement of Sonata in C (K.309); Beethoven, Second movement of Sonata Op. 13, the last movements of Op. 10, No. 3 and Op. 53; Schumann Arabeske Op. 18, Novelette in D major, Op. 21 No. 5.

The simple Rondo became linked with Sonata Form and was then called Sonata-Rondo (see p. 45).

CHAPTER FIVE

Sonata Form

The structure normally used for the first movement of a sonata, string quartet, symphony, or work of similar importance, is commonly known as sonata form or first-movement form. Neither name is particularly suitable. Sonata form is not the form of the whole sonata, but merely of one movement of it and, in addition, it is not confined to sonatas. On the other hand, the name 'first-movement form' does not cover all its uses, because it frequently appears in second and fourth movements. But the names are in common use and are accepted.* Sonata form grew out of binary, but as soon as it had developed far enough to be recognised as a distinct form, it had come to have three distinct sections.

The basic structure is set out below:

A¹ Exposition
- First subject-group in tonic
- Transition
- Second subject-group in dominant

B Development Section
- Modulatory section developing part of one or more themes or using new material

A² Recapitulation
- First subject-group in tonic
- Transition
- Second subject-group in tonic

The movement may begin with an introduction and end with a coda; but these features are not essential. The above table brings out the three-part form, but the historical link with binary form is clear also—the exposition ends in the dominant, and is

---

* Some writers describe sonata form as compound binary, and W. H. Hadow in Sonata Form (Novello 1896) calls it developed ternary, but students will find it less confusing not to use either of these descriptions.

usually marked by a repeat sign. The remaining part of the movement was also generally repeated.

The Evolution of Sonata Form. Look first at Ex. 22, the Menuet from Bach's French Suite No. 6. The first section, ending at bar 8, modulates to the dominant; the second section begins in the dominant, but at bar 16 the chord of B major is treated as the dominant in the key of E; bars 17–18 are identical with bars 1 and 2, and from then on the tonic key is emphasised to the end.

First Section

Bars 1–8   Theme in tonic modulating to dominant

Second Section

9–16 Beginning in dominant and modulating through C sharp minor back to tonic

17–24 Statement of opening in tonic continuing in tonic to the end.

Bars 17–24 can almost be regarded as a recapitulation in embryo and from that point of view the piece could divide into three equal sections.

Already binary form is tending towards ternary in its length and key scheme, but the contrast is still that of key and not of theme. In some binary movements—though not in the above Menuet—the two sections have similar endings. See Ex. 27 where bars 11 and 12 correspond to bars 5 and 6.

Ex. 27   Gottfried Grünewald, Gavotte

This binary feature is exploited on a larger scale in some sonatas where the exposition and recapitulation end similarly;

see for instance, C. P. E. Bach's 'Württemberg' Sonata No. 1 described on p. 31.

Characteristic features of sonata form are the second subject-group with the dominant as the main key, and the later appearance of the group in the tonic. In Ex. 22 and 27 there is nothing that can be called a second theme; but in both, and especially Ex. 27, there is a hint at the dominant-tonic relationship.

The sonatas and shorter pieces of A. Scarlatti give examples of a second theme. Although both themes have the same mood and the same rhythmical figures, the second is often distinctive enough to be recognized. The movements are still in obvious binary form but the themes in the second half of the first section, in the dominant key, are answered in the tonic in the second half of the second section. The well-known 'Pastorale'* is an example. As this is in the key of D minor, the second theme is in the relative major:

First Section

D minor	Bars 1– 8	First theme
F major	9–12	Scale passages
	13–27	Second theme

Second Section

F major, G minor	Bars 28–34	Extension of first theme
A minor (Tierce de picardie)		
D minor	35–39	Based on second theme
	40–61	An almost exact transposition of bars 5–27

In the sonatas of C. P. E. Bach and other composers of his generation, we find a further step in the evolution of sonata form. In brief, there are still two sections; but the second is much larger than the first and contains a recapitulation. The first movement of an early sonata of C. P. E. Bach, No. 1 in A minor of the 'Württemberg' Sonatas written in 1742, may be analysed as follows:

* Early Keyboard Music Vol. II, p. 136. Schirmer 1904.

First Section

Bars 1–9   Opening theme in A minor modu-
            lating to E minor.

9–20   Quotes the opening phrase in E
            minor and pursues a different course
            from 1–9, but keeps the dominant
            as the main key.

Second Section

21–41   Begins in C major with opening
            theme and modulates freely.

42–55   Quotes opening half-bar of theme in
            tonic, but bars 45–55 are a trans-
            position into A minor of bars 10–20.

There is a definite recapitulation (bars 42–55) but the same
theme serves both in the tonic and the dominant, that is, there is
no second subject-group.

As sonata form developed, contrast of theme became as
important as contrast of key. With a knowledge of the works
of Beethoven and Brahms, where contrast of mood is so strong,
it is difficult to think back to the time when a composer thought
it necessary only to contrast the key.

Another interesting feature of the sonata movement analysed
is that although the first section modulates to E minor, the second
section begins in C major. Here C. P. E. Bach uses both the
dominant minor and the relative major against the A minor tonic.

In the later works of C. P. E. Bach we find that the form is
more clearly defined; but as his sections in the dominant key
tend to consist of passage-work, they seldom contain a real
second subject. The first subject is still by far the most important
thematic element, and variety is obtained by modulation rather
than by contrast of theme.*

* In fact his opening melodies are so full of character that we are disappointed when
he does not follow them up in the way that Haydn and Mozart would have done. This
is a compliment to him, and because his work is so little known he has been underrated.
He has had to live in that no-man's land between the Bach-Handel and Haydn-Mozart
periods. He was not a contrapuntist like his father nor could he realise all the possibilities of
sonata form, but he was a poetical, sensitive composer and his works are worth studying.
Haydn and Mozart studied his works and Beethoven used his tutor to teach Czerny.

In the movements of Haydn we find that the section in the dominant key is generally a melodic one. It took him a little time to arrive at this. Formally, Haydn's early works are little more advanced than C. P. E. Bach's—there were only 18 years between them—but Haydn's genius for melody soon led him to replace C. P. E. Bach's passage-work by definite second subjects—memorable themes—in the dominant key. Even so, there is often no contrast of mood between the two themes; that did not become the rule until later.

The development of sonata form from the earlier binary movements is interesting because we can gradually see the essential difference making itself evident. The earlier movements are built on one theme that gradually unfolds itself, its mood varying little and all its growth generated from the opening few bars. Sonata form has two groups of melodies and the dramatic tension obtained from the interplay of these groups and the final resolution of their differences achieves unity in a different way.

This brief account of the development of sonata form would not be complete without a reference to the extraordinary anticipations in the works of J. S. Bach. Of these, the Prelude in D from the 48 Book II, is perhaps the most remarkable. It looks like a binary movement, with a double bar at the end of bar 16.

'J. S. Bach, Prelude in D, 48 Book II'

Exposition	Bars 1–5	First subject
	6–16	Second subject, mainly in dominant
Development	17–40	Modulating
Recapitulation	41–45	First subject adapted in bars 43–45
	46–56	Second subject—bars 6–16 transposed to the tonic, and slightly varied, with some of the parts interchanged.

Other works that can profitably be studied are the Sarabande of Partita IV, the Corrente of Partita VI, some of the Organ Sonatas, and the Prelude in B flat from the 48 Book II.

Having briefly traced the beginnings of sonata form we can examine it in more detail.

THE EXPOSITION

The first subject is sometimes preceded by an Introduction which is almost always slow. Introductions are commoner in orchestral than in chamber or solo works. Haydn often began his symphonies in this way, and Beethoven followed his example; Mozart seldom did, except in works such as the 'Linz' Symphony (K.425) which betray the influence of Haydn.

Introductions vary greatly in length; Beethoven Symphony No. 3 (*Eroica*) has only two loud tonic chords, whereas the introduction to the Seventh Symphony amounts almost to a movement in itself. The introduction to Sonata Op. 13 (*Pathétique*) is highly dramatic and is effectively used later in the movement.

First Subject-Group. The words 'Principal Subject' and 'Second Subject' are often used to describe the material appearing in the tonic and dominant keys respectively. This is misleading because it makes sonata form appear to have only two main themes. Although the first subject may be a short pithy phrase, it is not always so. Mozart Sonata in F (K.332) has twin subjects and Beethoven Sonata Op. 14 No. 1 contains at least three distinct ideas in the first twelve bars. As for the second subject-group it normally has two or more ideas or, as in Beethoven and Brahms, there is a large flow of themes in the dominant. So it is more accurate to use the description first subject-group and second subject-group.

Since the first subject-group is normally the composer's first contact with his listener he endeavours to make it as memorable as possible. Two common ways of achieving this are by writing a long melody that gradually builds up (Brahms's Fourth Symphony 1st movement) or by arresting the attention with a short pregnant phrase (Beethoven's Fifth Symphony 1st movement). A great composer can achieve much in a few notes and make a vivid impression on the listener who, if he is to follow the composer's argument, must remember the opening phrase. The first subject-group clearly establishes the tonic key although that does not preclude modulation. The end of the first subject-group is usually shown by a full or half cadence in the tonic.

Transition or Bridge Passage. After the first subject-group, the composer is faced with the necessity of modulating to the dominant for his second. The skill with which this is achieved is evidence of the composer's powers. In the best examples the first group leads inevitably to the second and virtue comes out of necessity. The transition can be short or long, or even non-existent. It can be built on the first subject-group or on new material. The obvious way is to extend the opening phrase and this is what often happens.

The methods used may be:

(1) To omit the transition and begin the second group straight away. This is sometimes done by Haydn and Mozart. The first subject-group has to end on the dominant and then the second group begins with the same chord and establishes the key. (Mozart Sonata in C K.330; Haydn Sonata No. 21 in C.).

(2) To repeat and develop the first subject-group, perhaps adding new material.
(Mozart, Sonata in A minor K.310 (bars 9–22); Haydn, Sonata No. 27 in G (bars 13–24); Beethoven Op. 10 No. 2 in F (bars 12–18)).

(3) To begin with new material and extend it but perhaps hark back to some of the first subject-group.
(Mozart, Sonata in F K.332 (bars 23–40); Haydn, Sonata No. 49 in E flat (bars 13–24); Beethoven, Sonata in E flat, Op. 31 No. 3 (bars 25–45)).

In the earlier examples of sonata form the second subject-group was well partitioned off from the first and in Haydn and Mozart we often have those formal scale and arpeggio passages which Wagner likened to the 'clatter of the dishes between the courses at a royal banquet'. As the form evolved, the tendency was to let the transition grow out of the opening and gradually merge into the second group. It is sometimes difficult to say where the transition begins. If one looks at the first subject-group in the recapitulation and compares it with the exposition, one finds the place where they begin to differ and this point would normally mark the beginning of the transition. In the same way, it is not always easy to decide where the transition ends and the second subject-group begins. A comparison with the recapitulation will again help. In the recapitulation the transition will vary so that the second subject-group will usually be an exact transposition to the tonic.

Second Subject-Group. Composers before Beethoven occasionally let the second subject-group be a repetition of the first subject-group in the key of the dominant. That this procedure can be effective is shown by the first movement of the 'Haffner' Symphony by Mozart (K.385), but normally the second group is longer than the first and contains several sections, one of which is usually a flowing melody. This is especially true of Beethoven who also makes his second group, or a section of it, contrast with the mood of the first. In a long second group, modulation of necessity must occur, but the principal key is never far away and the group ends with a closing section which reiterates the dominant key. Very often this last section is little more than a reiteration of the cadence and no new theme is presented. The simple decorative devices of broken chords and scales keep the issue of key clearly before the listener. So usual is this that this ending is called a 'codetta', but it must be understood that it is really all part of the second subject-group. The different rhythmical features of the various sections help to achieve contrast within the group, while the stability of the dominant tonal centre helps to achieve unity.

When a sonata is in a minor key the second group may be in the dominant minor or relative major. The latter is more common and the change of mode gives further variety.

Other keys have been used for the second group. Beethoven in his middle and late periods favoured the mediant, Sonata Op. 53 (*Waldstein*) and the submediant Sonata Op. 106 (*Hammerklavier*). There is no reason why there should be any restriction on the keys used, but the dominant for a movement in a major key and the relative major for a movement in a minor key were the most popular.

It was the custom for the exposition to be repeated and the composer either wrote a passage that would link the end of the exposition to the beginning, or he plunged straightway into his first subject again. The repeat, corresponding with the repeat in a binary movement, was common up to the time of Beethoven. He discarded the convention in the Sonata Op. 57 (*Appassionata*) and although he used it in some of his later sonatas one begins to feel it is unnecessary. In the days when Haydn and Mozart were 'contemporary composers' and the sonata was a comparatively new form, the repeat was helpful to the listener, who thus had a second chance to hear the tunes, but one may surmise that it was, even then, sometimes boring to the performer. It is difficult to traverse the same emotional route twice with equal fervour. To vary the interpretation as is sometimes done nowadays makes a virtue out of necessity, albeit in a questionable way.

To show the various divisions of the exposition, the first movements of two well-known Beethoven sonatas are analysed.

Sonata in F minor, Op. 2 No. 1

First subject-group	Bars 1–8, all generated from the opening two bars, ending on a half-close.
Transition	Bars 9–20 built on the first subject starting in C minor and modulating to E flat, which is eventually treated as the dominant of the second subject-group.
Second subject-group	20–40 Key A flat major. The opening theme generates a figure (bar 25), which in its turn generates another (bar 32). Although the group is continuous, there are three ideas present.
	41–48 A new two-bar phrase, repeated and augmented, confirming the key.

Sonata in C minor, Op. 13 (*Pathétique*)

Introduction	1–10 built on the material in the opening bar and ending on a dominant pedal.

First subject-group	11–25 built on an 8-bar theme (extended to 9 by overlap).
Transition	25–40 based on the first subject-group and on a rising semitone pedal, 4 bars on G, 3 on A flat, 1 on A natural, 8 on B flat, which is the dominant of the first section of the second subject-group.
Second subject-group	(i) 41–78 E flat minor, modulating and eventually reaching the normal key of E flat major at 77 (the use of E flat minor is unusual).
	(ii) 79–102 A new theme in E flat overlapping to
	(iii) 103–110 Another new theme in E flat overlapping to repetition of part of the first subject in E flat and then leading back to the repeat.

THE DEVELOPMENT SECTION

As the name implies, this is the section where the composer develops the themes stated in the exposition. The word is misleading, for it implies that there is development here and none elsewhere. The best examples of sonata form show a continuous development of musical ideas from the first bar to the last. Apart from the development section proper, sonata form contains much development. The transition is often a development of the first subject-group and the various sections of the second subject-group often grow out of each other.

Although development is the purpose of this section, it also presents an opportunity for the composer to get away from the tonic and dominant keys that prevail in the exposition. In fact he often avoids these keys.

But what is musical development? It is the creation of something new from what has already been heard. Melodic, rhythmic or harmonic ideas already presented may be so manipulated as to generate new ideas. To illustrate this, part of the development section of Beethoven's Sonata Op. 2 No. 1 will be examined.

Beethoven, Sonata in F minor, Op. 2, No. 1
1st movement, bars 20–22

Ex. 28

Ex. 28 shows part of the second subject which is to be developed.

In the exposition it appears in A flat major, but it first appears in the development section transposed to B flat minor (bar 55). It is repeated in C minor (bar 63). The first development shows a short tag added in the treble (second and third beats of bar 69). The right hand of Ex. 28 becomes the left hand of Ex. 29.

the same
bars 67–69

Ex. 29

This is repeated sequentially (Ex. 30).

Ex. 30 which is a continuation of Ex. 29 shows a sequential repetition (bars 70 and 71) in key of B flat minor.

At the next repetition (bars 72–73) the ending is delayed. The crotchets a′ natural and b′ flat (bar 71) are answered by the minims g′ and a′ flat (bars 73, 74). The bass is pushed off its old course by the delayed treble and becomes syncopated. This new idea is carried on sequentially. (Ex. 30)

In Ex. 30 can be seen something new growing out of something old. If we were given the last few bars it would be well-nigh impossible to work out its origin, and yet as the music proceeds the development is logical and interesting.

There are innumerable ways of developing a theme. Some of the most common present the old theme in new guises. The major

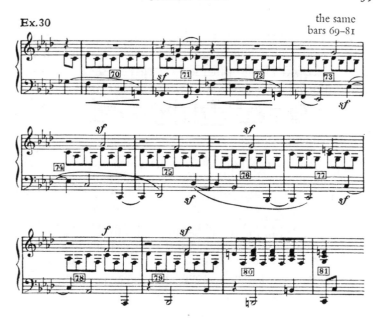

theme may become minor or vice versa, the harmonies accompanying the theme may be changed, the theme may be augmented or diminished or it may be used as a subject for contrapuntal treatment.

Sometimes a new theme is introduced into the development section. The new material is known as an episode. Mozart often does this, as in the first movement of Sonatas in D (K.284); B flat (K.333); G (K.283). One of the best known examples is in the first movement of Symphony No. 3 (*Eroica*) of Beethoven, but see also the first movement of his pianoforte sonatas Op. 10 No. 2; Op. 14 No. 1.

Towards the end of the development section the composer has to prepare the way back for the recapitulation. He must return to the tonic and although the journey is obligatory the music that takes us there should sound inevitable. This is one of the most interesting structural points in the movement, and the student should examine many movements and see the various ways in which the problem can be solved.

THE RECAPITULATION

The third part of sonata form unifies the movement by re-establishing the tonic as the tonal centre. The exposition has a small section in the tonic and a larger in the dominant, the development ranges through other keys and at last stability comes as the recapitulation insists on the tonic. The second subject-group as well as the first is in that key. As a rule the transition between them is altered. As a modulatory link is not needed at this point, it may be omitted, as in Beethoven Op. 10 No. 2, but this is not usual. This is probably because the entry of the second subject-group is more striking when preceded by subordinate transitional matter. Sometimes the transition remains unaltered; if it ends on the dominant in the exposition (leading to a second subject in the dominant), it can equally well be repeated in the recapitulation (leading to a second subject in the tonic). But this, again, is unusual; though there is an example in Haydn Sonata in C, No. 21.

Normally, however, the transition is altered; its modulations are changed to make the appearance of the second subject in the tonic sound as strong as its first appearance in the dominant. In a movement in C major, in the exposition the transition might end on a chord of D major, the dominant of G; in the recapitulation the transition would end on a chord of G major, the dominant of C. An example of the normal procedure will be found in Beethoven Sonata in E, Op. 14 No. 1 analysed at the end of this chapter.

The modulations that took place during the course of the second subject-group are presented in the recapitulation, but with the tonic as centre. If the second subject-group has been in a key other than the dominant the procedure varies. The very fact of having a second subject-group in an unusual key shows that the form is comparatively free and leads one to expect something different in the recapitulation. A well-known example is the Sonata in C major Op. 53 (*Waldstein*) by Beethoven where the second subject is in E major in the exposition. In the recapitulation, it begins in A major and modulates through A minor to C major, where it remains.

In a movement in a minor key the second subject-group in the relative major may be put either in the tonic minor or tonic major in the recapitulation. When it is put in the minor, as is often done by Mozart, we have a change in the character of the theme. The first movement of the G minor symphony (K.550) by Mozart shows this. The second subject-group is in B flat major in the exposition and in G minor in the recapitulation. The practice of later composers is to preserve the original mode by using the tonic major.

Since the main object of the recapitulation is to establish the tonic key, we find that composers regard this as more important than repeating the exposition exactly. Very often the recapitulation is shortened by omitting a section, perhaps because the material has been worked in the development section, or perhaps because the composer feels that his argument can now be compressed. The composer does not set out to keep rules and it is not possible to list all variants in the recapitulation. But what is described above, with a few other variants is set out below:

(1) The transition may be omitted (Beethoven Sonata in F Op. 10 No. 2).
(2) The transition may be kept exactly (Haydn Sonata in B flat No. 41).
(3) The first subject may appear in the subdominant (Schubert Symphony No. 5 in B flat; Mozart Sonata in C, K.545).
(4) First subject-group may be omitted (Brahms Symphony No. 1 last movement; Chopin Sonata in B flat minor Op. 35).
(5) Second subject-group may precede the first (Mozart Sonata in D, K.311).

THE CODA

The coda (literally tail-piece) began as a reinforcing of the tonic key; simple examples can be found in Mozart and Haydn. In Mozart's Sonata in C, (K.283) last movement, it is the chord of the dominant seventh followed by the tonic. In the slow movement of the same sonata it is a re-harmonisation of the opening two bars. With Mozart and Haydn it rarely assumed real importance, but from Beethoven onwards it became a structural necessity. Beethoven often used it to make almost a fourth section to sonata form, sometimes introducing new material. Beethoven's Symphony No. 3 (*Eroica*) has a coda of 135 bars, and in his Sonata Op. 81a the coda equals in length the development and recapitulation together. Since the purpose of the coda is to sum up what has gone before, there is no set plan of construction.

To conclude, a complete sonata movement by Beethoven is analysed.

Sonata in E, Op. 14 No. 1

Exposition First subject-group 1–12	Bars 1–4 Theme on tonic pedal with rising fourths (minims) as the motive. 5–12 Another theme in semiquavers for 2 bars, followed by one in quavers.
Transition 13–22	built on the opening four bars and from 17–22 on a pedal F sharp, leading to
Second subject-group 23–60 in B major	Section (a) 23–38 Four 4-bar phrases. (b) 39–46 Two 4-bar phrases. (c) 46–57 A four-bar phrase followed by one of six bars overlapping to (d) 57–61 Four-bar reiteration of cadence (codetta).
Development 61–90	Bars 61–64 built on bars 1–4; followed by an episode 65–81 in A minor, modulating to C major and reaching B as a pedal point. 81–90 on a pedal B (dominant of E) built on bars 1–4.
Recapitulation First subject-group 91–102	Same as bars 1–12 except that the accompaniment is changed from repeated chords to scales.
Transition 103–113	In the exposition this began in the tonic key, but the cadence 102–103 is interrupted, so that 103 is a chord of C major.

The scales introduced at 91 are continued. Bars 107–113 are on a pedal B and are a transposition of 17–22.

Second subject-group 114–end

11–147 is the same as 23–56 but now in the tonic key. 148 and 149 are the same as 57 and 58 but the original four-bar phrase is expanded into a

Coda

148–155 an eight-bar phrase overlapping with 155–162, another eight-bar phrase. Built on the opening rising fourths.

Chapter Six

Varied Types of Sonata Form

1. *Abridged Sonata Form (or Modified Sonata Form)*

The name implies that the structure is smaller than sonata form. Briefly, it is sonata form with the development section replaced by a chord or a few bars that link the end of the exposition to the recapitulation. Ternary form is in fact changed to a type of binary by the omission of the middle section, but not to the older binary, as will be seen from the plan set out.

A { First subject in tonic.
Transition.
Second subject in dominant.

A modulation from dominant to tonic either by a dominant seventh chord or by a short phrase leading to

B { First subject in tonic.
Transition.
Second subject in tonic.
Coda (if necessary).

It will be seen that the themes are described as first and second subjects, the word 'group' that was used in the previous chapter having been omitted. This is because the movements are shorter and do not generally need more than two distinct themes.

The form is often used for the slow movement of a sonata or symphony. The movement generally takes a shorter time to play than the allegro first movement and, since it is in slow time, there is no need for length in the subjects. They are often of a lyrical nature and less dramatic than those of a first movement. Because of the simplicity of the themes and their slow speed they are often varied in the recapitulation.

This form was used for many operatic overtures in the early nineteenth century by Rossini and others. The popular overtures *The Barber of Seville*, *La Scala di Seta*, *Semiramide*, are in this form.

44

In classical music, examples are the slow movements of Beethoven Sonatas Op. 2 No. 1; Op. 10 No. 1; Op. 31 No. 2, and 'Prometheus' Overture; Mozart Overture to *Figaro* and the slow movement Sonata in F (K.332).

The second movement of Beethoven's Sonata in C minor Op. 10 No. 1 is analysed below:

A	Bars 1–16	First subject in A flat major.
	17–23	Transition.
	24–44	Second subject in dominant.
	45	Dominant 7th chord of A flat major leading to
B	46–61	First subject in tonic, varied.
	62–70	Transition extended, leading to
	71–91	Second subject in tonic.
	91–112	Coda.

2. *Sonata-Rondo Form or Modern Rondo Form*

As the name indicates, the form combines elements of sonata form and old rondo form. Both are set out below for comparison:

Sonata-Rondo	*Old Rondo*
A^1 Principal rondo theme Transition leading to	A^1 Principal rondo theme
B^1 Second theme in dominant	B Episode, usually in dominant
A^2 Principal theme in tonic	A^2 Return of principal theme
C Episode; possibly some development	C Second episode, usually in a relative key
A^3 Principal theme in tonic Transition leading to	A^3 Return of principal theme Coda (possibly).
B^2 Second theme in tonic	
A^4 Final appearance of principal theme and/or a coda in which principal theme appears.	

Comparing the two forms, the episode (B) in the old rondo and the second theme in sonata-rondo have the same function, i.e. they make a contrasting section to the first theme. They both have the first return of the principal theme A². The episode C in old rondo is usually a contrasting theme of about the same length and importance as the other sections. In sonata-rondo, episode C may be (a) purely an episode or (b) partly episode and partly development or (c) all development. The A3 and coda of the old rondo is expanded in sonata-rondo to a recapitulation in which the second theme appears in the tonic key. The essential feature of the rondo structure, the periodic appearance of the main theme, is further reinforced by the fourth statement of it.

The form is often used for last movements of classical works, including concertos. It is suitable as it has some affinity with sonata form and thus gives cohesion to the complete sonata. Its themes are generally simple and because of the lack of development they follow each other quicker and create a sense of melodic spontaneity.

Stewart Macpherson* says that 'This form, foreshadowed by Mozart and Haydn, reaches its most assured and perfect shape in the works of Beethoven, in whose sonatas there are many instances of this particular design.' This perhaps does not quite do justice to Mozart and Haydn. In the Mozart concertos and sonatas there are many interesting varieties of the sonata-rondo. Sonatas in A minor (K.310); D (K.311) and (K.576); B flat (K.333); in F (K.533 and 494) should be examined. These are not all exactly on the plan outlined above, but the general idea is the same.†

One of these movements is analysed and also a Haydn movement and then a more normal Beethoven example:

Mozart Sonata in F (K.533 and 494) last movement

A¹ Bars   1–12   Principal rondo theme
B   13–34   Second theme in dominant (Bars 13–18 could be taken as a transition as they are omitted in the recapitulation, but 13 begins immediately in dominant.)

---

* Form in Music (J. Williams 1915).

† With the possible exception of K.576, a most interesting movement. Most of the themes grow out of the opening phrase. It is easy to divide into sections but difficult to name. Hadow in his book *Sonata Form* calls it sonata form with a repetition of the first subject preceding the development; Morris in *The Structure of Music* calls it a rondo with developments instead of episodes, and I incline to the latter's view.

	35–38	A short link leading to
A²	39–50	Principal theme in tonic (varied)
C	51–79	Episode in D minor and B flat major (the minor section has a reference to the principal theme)
	79–82	A short link leading to
A³	83–94	Principal theme in tonic, varied, but different from A²
D	95–116	Episode in F minor
	117–119	A short link leading to
A⁴	120–131	Principal theme in tonic, still further varied
B²	132–151	Second theme in tonic. Bars 132–142 are an ornamental version of 19–29, but 143–151 break away and rise to a climax on the chord of the German sixth.
	152–187	Coda, in which the rhythm and shape of the principal theme are treated contrapuntally.

This movement has an extra episode (D) and consequentially another appearance of the principal theme. This is not uncommon with Mozart who, Hadow says, 'did for the Rondo what Haydn did for the Minuet'. He would be a rash person who would say that the above was in any way inferior to the form as shown in Beethoven Op. 14 No. 1 analysed below. Beethoven may be easier to analyse, but that does not mean that his music is better. The final answer to any question of form is in the sound of the music. If it sounds logical—that is, if it has the two virtues of unity and variety—the theorist must include it as formally good, whether it fits a preconceived plan or not.

Haydn's symphonies and sonatas give a variant of the form. In the chapter on sonata form attention was drawn to the fact that in Haydn and Mozart the second subject was sometimes a transposition to the dominant of the first subject. The emphasis was on the change of key. This was not due to inability on the part of the composers to think of another theme but was of their own deliberate choosing. It was not something that occurred in their early works and which they grew out of, because we find it among their later works as well. This pursuing of one subject gives the music a sense of onward movement and was much used by Haydn in his rondos. The subjects are simple, lightly accompanied melodies and they are often treated in a mildly contrapuntal way which adds to the excitement without losing buoyancy.

As an example the last movement of Haydn's Sonata No. 48 in C is analysed (the themes are quoted):

A^1 Bars	1–30	Principal rondo theme; the first phrase (6 bars) is quoted (Ex.31). This section is in binary form since bars 1–12 and 13–30 are both repeated; but the opening theme returns in tonic (bars 21–30) with a different ending.
	31–52	Development of the principal theme, leading to
B	53–91	First episode in G major which begins in the same way as the principal theme and develops it (Ex. 32).
A^2	92–122	Principal theme in tonic (a shortened form).
C	122–173	Second episode in C minor (Ex. 33) the theme has a rhythmic connection with the principal theme and develops the semitonal movement (Ex. 34) of bars 2 and 3 (Ex. 31) and later quotes the opening in E flat (bar 154) (Ex. 35).
A^3	174–220	Principal theme in tonic slightly varied and shortened. Developed and leading to
B^2	221–255	Almost a replica of 53–87. Here the opening uses more notes and is ff instead of f in the tonic key.
	255–263	Coda in principal theme.

The episode C being in the minor key makes a contrast with the remainder. Since B is reminiscent of A, when B^2 comes in the tonic key it has the effect of a grand affirmation of all that has gone before. The movement is built on one theme but from the point of view of key it can be called sonata-rondo. One must remember that Haydn, if he had wanted to, could have written contrasting themes, but a quick movement of this type sounds most exciting with its insistence on the single time-pattern.

Ex.31
Presto

Haydn, Sonata No. 48 in C major
2nd movement, bars 1–6

Ex.32

the same
bars 53–59

Ex.33

the same
bars 122 –126

Ex.34

the same
bars 148–154

Ex.35

the same
bars 154–156

Beethoven Op. 14 No. 1 (last movement)

A¹ Bars 1–8 Principal rondo theme in key E.

9–21 Repetition of theme and transition.

B¹ 22–30 Second subject in B major.

A² 30–38 Principal theme in tonic.

39–47 Principal theme in tonic minor providing a link to

C 47–83 Episode in G major reaching a pedal point on the note B (the dominant of E) at bar 76.

A³ 84–91 Principal theme in tonic.

92–98 Transition leading to

B²   99–108 Second subject in subdominant (unusual feature).

A4   109–131 Return of principal theme syncopated and moving into a coda.

One of the features of Beethoven's movements in sonata form is the contrasting mood of the subjects. In his rondo movements also he contrasts the main theme with the episodes and thus brings a sense of drama to the structure. There are examples where he replaced the central episode by development (last movements of Sonatas in B flat Op. 22; G Op. 31 No. 1; E minor Op. 90).

CHAPTER SEVEN

The Complete Sonata

The word sonata describes a musical composition of some importance usually in three or four movements either for a solo instrument or for two instruments. When the same type of composition is for more than two instruments, the title of sonata is no longer used, but one describing the number and sometimes the nature of the instruments. A pianoforte trio is a sonata for piano, violin and 'cello, and a string quartet a sonata for two violins, viola and 'cello. As the groups get larger so the name changes to quintet, sextet, septet, octet, nonet; after this the word symphony is generally used. So a symphony is a sonata for orchestra. What is said in this chapter about the sonata as a whole will apply equally to the combinations mentioned above. For ease of reference, examples will be chosen from pianoforte music in the main, but the student should analyse chamber music and symphonies as well.

There are usually three or four movements. The first an allegro movement, almost always in sonata form, the second a slow movement often of a lyrical character, the third a dance movement, and the fourth, one that will balance the first but often less serious. When there are three movements the dance is generally omitted. There are many departures from the above, but it is the average plan.

First Movement

Except in a few isolated instances, sonata form is used. (The alternative name is first-movement form.) The listener's ear is fresh and the composer tries to establish contact in as memorable a way as possible. When one thinks of a sonata or a symphony, it is usually the first movement that comes to mind.

Second Movement

The second or slow movement makes a contrast with the first allegro movement, and sonata form would be out of place here where the mood is more relaxed. Also the slow speed would make sonata form interminably long. It is used occasionally by Haydn and Mozart, but it is rare in Beethoven (Symphony No. 2 in D; Sonata in B flat Op. 22).

The forms most frequently used are:

(a) Ternary (Mozart Sonata in C K.309; Beethoven Sonata in G Op. 79; Brahms Clarinet Quintet).

(b) Abridged sonata form (Mozart Sonata in F K.332; Beethoven Sonatas in F minor Op. 2 No. 1; C minor Op. 10 No. 1; D minor Op. 31 No. 2).

(c) Air and variations (see Chapter Fourteen).

Not so frequently used in piano music (Beethoven Sonata for violin and piano Op. 47; Haydn Emperor Quartet Op. 76 No. 3).

(d) Old rondo (Mozart Sonata in C minor K.457; C major K.545; Beethoven Sonata in A Op. 2 No. 2; Sonata in C minor Op. 13 *Pathétique*).

Third Movement

This is usually a minuet and trio or scherzo and trio. Its form has been discussed in chapter four but reference must be made to Haydn's attitude to the Minuet. His minuets were vivacious and sparkling and different from the older dance. Although they were minuets in name they were scherzos in spirit. Haydn uses the word scherzando as early as Op. 3 No. 6 and the prevailing mood of his music, except when he is being serious, may well be described by this word. Although Haydn livened up the minuet, it was Beethoven who really established the scherzo and his third movement is often called scherzo and trio. He did not always keep the gay mood of the scherzo and he lets the movement depict any mood he chooses. The third movements of symphonies 5, 6 and 7 establish three quite different moods.

The scherzo and trio has the same structure as the minuet and trio. However in the symphonies the trio is sometimes played again followed by the scherzo (giving the formula ABABA) as in Beethoven Symphony No. 7 in A major. Mozart in the Clarinet Quintet (K.581) and Dvořák in the 'New World' Symphony write a minuet with two trios (ABACA).

Fourth Movement

This is generally in old rondo, sonata-rondo, or sonata form.

(a) Sonata-rondo Beethoven Op. 22, Op. 26, Op. 28; Mozart Sonata in A minor (K.310); Brahms Violin Concerto, Op. 77 and Pianoforte Concertos in D minor, Op. 15 and B flat major, Op. 83.

(b) Old rondo Mozart Sonata in F (K.533 and 494); Beethoven Op. 10 No. 3.

(c) Sonata form Beethoven Op. 10 No. 1 and 2, Op. 27 No. 2; Mozart Sonata in G (K.283).

Occasionally there is a set of variations. Beethoven, Symphony No. 3 (*Eroica*) and Brahms Symphony No. 4 are two well-known instances in orchestral music and Beethoven Sonata in E Op. 109 and Mozart Sonata in D (K.284) in piano music.

Although the above list of forms for each movement gives the normal procedure, music does not thrive on normality, and there are many works which differ from the above. The music of Haydn has many examples. It must be remembered that his early works date from 1755-56, and they show the transitional state of the sonata. For instance, in the twelve works usually known as String Quartets, Op. 1 and 2, eleven have five movements. But in Op. 3 we find the number reduced to four, to which he normally kept from then on. In his symphonies we find similar variety. The last movement of his first symphony is in the early sonata form, in which the two sections are repeated (as found in C. P. E. Bach); in the second it is old rondo; in the third it is built on three themes given out at the beginning which make triple counterpoint; in the fourth a minuet in the early sonata form; in the fifth a very short presto (59 bars) in binary form. When one gets to Nos. 6, 7, 8 ('Le Matin', 'Le Midi', and 'Le Soir') one finds elements of the concerto form present with concertante parts for solo violin and 'cello. In Le Midi there is a movement headed recitative which foreshadows Beethoven Op. 31 No. 2 in D minor, written more than 40 years later. The last seven bars are given in Ex. 36.

Ex. 36   Haydn, Symphony No. 7 in C major (*Le Midi*)
Adagio   2nd movement, bars 23–29

Solo Violin

Strings

The movement is 30 bars long and has a neutral key-signature beginning in C minor and ending in B minor.

Haydn was composing during the whole of the second half of the eighteenth century and into the nineteenth. He was eighteen when J. S. Bach died and he lived another eighteen years after Mozart's death. His music covers a wide span and is itself a lesson in the development of form.

Sometimes the movements of a sonata or symphony may be linked together; this can be found occasionally from C. P. E. Bach onwards. A well-known example is the joining of the third and fourth movements of Beethoven's Fifth Symphony. Another device to unify the structure is to use the same theme, or a variant of it, in more than one movement. In chapter twelve this device is shown in the works of Frescobaldi (1583–1643) and it was a recognized method at this period; but it seems then to have been neglected until we get 'L'idée fixe' that appears in the *Symphonie Fantastique* of Berlioz. This 'idée fixe' (literally *fixed idea*) is a theme whose main musical shape remains constant, although the note-lengths, rhythm and orchestration vary. It appears in all the movements, and is intended to serve as a link between them. In practice however it does not do so because the theme is short and not very distinctive.

Liszt in the *Faust* Symphony carries this idea still further. The three movements headed Faust, Gretchen and Mephistopheles depict these three characters; the second movement uses themes from the first, and the third uses themes from the first two. In fact, most of the themes for Mephistopheles are different versions of the 'Faust' themes.

César Franck is another example of a composer using a theme in more than one movement. In the Symphony in D minor the Theme of Faith is the common factor between the first and last movements, and in its blazing orchestration it can hardly be overlooked. The last movement also uses a theme from the second. Because of this use of themes the work is said to be in cyclic form, presumably because the 'cycle' is completed when the opening themes come again at the end. This method is common in César Franck's large-scale works and he is regarded as the establisher of this form.

The 'L'idée fixe' originating in Berlioz gave rise to the 'leit-motiv' of Wagner. Unity is given to his operas, especially those comprising the Ring, by the use of themes depicting persons or ideas. Dramatic necessity requires that certain themes are related to others. A new theme also may develop from an existing one.

In a further effort to unify the whole work rather than create individual movements, a sonata or symphony may be in one movement. Variety will still be present and the work will be no shorter, but the last section strives to become a logical outcome of the first.

A development during the second half of the nineteenth century from the descriptive symphonies mentioned above by Berlioz and Liszt was the symphonic poem or tone poem. The 'Faust' Symphony is really 'programme music', that is, it is music which relies on something outside its own art for inspiration. It still retains the title of symphony, but when the composer writes something 'programmatic' in one movement, the composition is known as a symphonic poem or tone poem. Sometimes the composer gives us a synopsis of the story so that we know what the various sections are intending to portray. Like a symphony there are many themes and their development is of great importance. Liszt was the pioneer in this field and wrote, amongst others, *Les Préludes*, *Tasso*, *Mazeppa*. Richard Strauss with *Don Juan*, *Death and Transfiguration*, *Till Eulenspiegel* etc. was the composer most popularly associated with the symphonic poem.

SONATINA

A sonatina is literally a small sonata. Some sonatinas are important works, but only called so because they occupy less time than a sonata. Others are smaller in musical stature. The lighter type of sonatina is represented by Clementi and Kuhlau and the more important type by Ravel and Busoni. However, the title is not always a sure guide. There are some sonatinas which could justly be called sonatas and vice versa.

CHAPTER EIGHT

The Concerto

If one were asked to describe the form of a concerto, one would first have to find out to what period in musical history the questioner was referring. The word 'concerto' (literally 'accord together') like the words sonata and symphony, has been in use for over 300 years, and its meaning has not remained constant; but in common with sonata and symphony it refers to a complete work in a number of movements.

The difference between the concerto and the sonata or symphony is that in the former the composer divides his forces, one relatively weak in tone and the other relatively strong. One of the ways of obtaining variety in music is by the use of different degrees of volume—the 'echo' effect is one of the oldest devices in composition. Whereas in the symphony and sonata this is one of many devices employed, in the concerto it pervades the whole of the form, and the chief interest comes from the way in which the composer marshals the opposing forces. It is true therefore to say that the principle of the concerto is that of contrast of sound, and the composer is judged by his ability to exploit this and at the same time demonstrate the overriding principle of unity that is necessary in every work of art.

In the Bach-Handel period the forces were not too disparate, often a group of 3 or 4 orchestral leaders contrasting with the rest of the orchestra. As the latter might number no more than a dozen or so, and the players were less proficient, the difference in volume would not have been very great. In this period concertos were already being written for one solo instrument, and from this time onward the single soloist is the rule. There were many reasons for the change, such as the rise of virtuosity, the increase in the sonority of the instruments, the replacing of the harpsichord

by the pianoforte, and the love of the public (and we may
guess of some players also) for instrumental display. These
factors definitely affect the concerto from the second half of the
eighteenth century onwards.

The first picture that would come into the ordinary person's
mind today if the word concerto was mentioned, would be of a
pianist valiantly striving against rather overwhelming odds in
works by Tchaikovsky or Grieg. Yet it is amazing how the
seemingly unequal combat of one against eighty or so comes out
in performance. The modern concert grand with its violently
percussive sounds can force its way through a vast amount of
orchestral tone. Moreover, the listener's eyes are apt to be focused
on the hands of the player rather than on the orchestra, and this
probably helps the ear. The position of the instrument on the
platform is a further asset. There is no doubt that the factor of
display has a very important place, and a concerto without a
cadenza would not be kindly looked upon by the average
concert-goer.

It is convenient to examine the concerto under four headings:
>   The origins of the concerto
>   The Bach-Handel period
>   The classical concerto
>   Later developments.

The Origins of the Concerto

The earliest use of the word concerto has hardly any relation
to the later developments; it is used in its literal meaning of
'combined effort', when a group of players or singers was added
to an already existing group. The Italian composer Viadana
(1564–1627) uses the word to describe a number of motets
employing solo voices and instruments. His *Cento Concerti
Ecclesiastici* were published in Venice in 1602.*

The 'combined effort' sense persisted till Bach (certain cantatas
are called concertos). But by then it was more or less obsolete.
The word had come to mean an instrumental work of the type

* One of them is quoted in HAM 185.

developed by such Italians as Torelli (1650–1708), Corelli (1653–1713), A. Scarlatti (1659–1725), Vivaldi (1680–1743), and taken up by Bach and Handel. Bach arranged a number of Italianate concertos for the organ and other keyboard instruments. He seems to have been chiefly influenced by Vivaldi, whose music, after a long period of neglect, is now beginning to be enjoyed for its own sake.

The concerto of about 1700 was a work in perhaps as many as six or seven movements, of all shapes and sizes; link passages consisting of a few block chords: elaborately ornamented melodies with simple accompaniments: binary movements, da capo movements, more or less closely modelled on familiar dance-types and fugues. There is also, as a rule, at least one movement in ritornello form. None of these forms was confined to the concerto—they were also used in arias, choruses, chamber sonatas, and solo keyboard music—but as the ritornello form seems to have been developed chiefly by the Italian concerto composers, it is described here. The movement analysed below—from Torelli's 'Concerti Grossi', Op. 8 published at Bologna in 1709—is typical.*

A^1 Bars 1–16 First section, played full, containing two themes; (a) bars 1–10 Key C minor, (Ex. 37) and (b) bars 11–16 key B flat (Ex. 38) modulating to G minor.

B   17–26 A new theme for the soloist with a figured bass accompaniment (Ex. 39) in key G minor modulating many times and eventually reaching E flat major.

A^2 26–34 Return of first section played full in the key of E flat major and modulating to F minor.

C   34–46 Another new theme for the soloist (Ex. 40) in F minor with figured bass accompaniment modulating to C minor.

A^3 47–63 Repeat of bars 1–16 but remaining in tonic key.

     64–66 A coda made by repetition of bars 61–63.

* Quoted in HAM 246.

Torelli, Concerto Grosso, Op. 8, No. 8
Last movement, bars 1–4

Ex.37

the same
bars 11–12

Ex.38

the same
bar 17

Ex.39

the same
bars 34–36

Ex.40

The formula is A¹BA²CA³, A being the principal section played by all the players, and B and C the sections played by the soloist. This formula is the same as old rondo form and one would assume from this example that the concerto movement and the rondo were identical. Although this example was chosen to emphasise the similarity, in other examples there are differences, but in all there is the common feature of a periodic return of the opening section. The likeness to rondo is self-evident but the main differences may be listed as follows:

(a) In old rondo there are usually two further appearances of the principal rondo theme after the opening one, but the concerto is more free and there may be three or more. In between each there would be a section for the soloist or solo-group.

(b) The repetitions of the opening section are, except for the last, generally in a key other than the tonic.

(c) Most important of all in old rondo the episodes are thematically contrasted with the rondo theme, but in the concerto the corresponding sections may use the opening theme or may be new themes or may be a mixture of both. Although this may appear monotonous, there is always the variety of sound due to the contrasting groups of players.

The section that keeps returning is called by that name in Italian 'ritornello', and the word is applied to all the variants of the form which have as their common factor repetitions of the opening section in various keys. Sometimes the repeat is in full and at other times shortened or varied, but the last normally matches the first in length.

The Bach-Handel Period

The form outlined above was used greatly in the music of the first half of the eighteenth century and the principal examples in use today are in the music of Bach and Handel. They used it for vocal as well as instrumental music, in fact in most music where there were two forces to be reconciled. The form proved itself suitable for any combination of voices and instruments. 'Concerto grosso' was the name given to the instrumental form.

Handel's 'Concerti Grossi' and an air such as 'Thou shalt break them' (*Messiah*), Bach's 'Brandenburg' Concertos and the opening chorus and most of the solos in the B Minor Mass are in ritornello form. It was not used for all the movements of the concerto. There was no rule about the matter nor was there uniformity over the number of movements. Bach seems generally to have preferred three, but Handel often uses more. The ritornello form was not so much used for the slower movements, but often used for the quicker. The music for the solo or solo-group is called 'solo' or 'concertante' and the larger chorus group is called 'ripieno'.

The best way to show the variants of the form is to analyse examples; on the following pages are two arias, a movement from Bach's 'Brandenburg' No. 4 and the opening chorus of a Bach cantata.

Deposuit potentes (Magnificat) Bach, Key F sharp minor

A¹ Bars   1–14   Opening orchestral ritornello ending with perfect cadence in tonic.

B   15–27   Tenor entry quoting bars 1–8 of the ritornello whilst the ritornello uses a new figure. Modulation to A major.

A²   27–35   Ritornello in A major ending with a perfect cadence.

C   35–54   Tenor entry in A major modulating through B minor to F sharp minor. Some new material, but four bars previously heard are exactly quoted.

A³   54–67   Repeat of opening ritornello in tonic key.

The aria has immense vigour and its strong falling phrases picture 'He hath put down the mighty from their seat'.

'*Thou shalt break them*' (*Messiah*) Handel, Key A minor

A¹ Bars   1–10   Orchestral ritornello in A minor with a perfect cadence.

         11–15   Entry of soloist with a different theme from ritornello. The ritornello is repeated but varied to accommodate the solo, still in A minor.

B   15–30   Repeat of three bars of opening; the soloist enters and the ritornello theme is developed, modulating to a full close in Key C.

A²   30–35   Shortened form of ritornello in C major.

C   35–65   Entry of soloist against ritornello theme with modulation, but with A minor still as principal key. The climax is reached with the soloist's highest note and the ritornello's most intense phrase.

A³   65–74   Repetition of orchestral ritornello bars 1–10.

The interplay of ritornello and solo is of a very high order, the ritornello is pushed into the background when the soloist has florid phrases. The themes of both parts accentuate the meaning of the words.

Brandenburg Concerto No. 4 in G, Bach (last movement)

The solo group consists of a violin and two flutes; the ripieno, the usual strings. This movement shows that the concerto form had a link with fugue (*q.v.*) as well as with rondo. The age was a contrapuntal one and the solo group and the ripieno share in the prevailing fugato* style.

A¹ Bars 1–41 Ripieno		Ritornello. The violas announce a four-bar subject accompanied by the bass, which is answered fugally by the second violins. Subject and answer again appear. The flutes enter in unison with the answer and the ritornello ends with a perfect cadence in the tonic key.
B Bars 42–67 Solo Group		The opening theme of the ritornello is played by the flutes in stretto with a continuous quaver movement on the violin. The key veers toward D major and the ripieno violins enter in imitation leading to
A² Bars 67–88 Ripieno		Ritornello in D major, the orchestra making use of the quaver figure introduced in section B by the solo violin. Modulates to a full close in E minor.
C Bars 88–127 Solo violin		A quaver figure derived from section B very lightly accompanied. Semiquavers gradually introduced until the violin is playing a bravura solo entirely in semiquavers almost in the style of a later cadenza.
A³ Bars 127–159 Ripieno		Ritornello in E minor modulating to a full close in D.
D Bars 159–175 Flutes alone		The two flutes play the main theme ornamented and there is a modulation to C major.
A⁴ Bars 176–244 Ripieno		Ritornello in C major for seven bars during which the flutes enter and link to Ritornello in tonic which becomes a full version of section B (Bars 193–202 = 42–52) but instead of veering towards D major the same material

* For the meaning of this as well as other terms used in fugue the reader should consult the index and the chapter on Fugue.

is in Key G. The D major ritornello at bar 67 is answered by one in G at bar 207. A tonic pedal foreshadows the end, but the contrapuntal movement is suddenly stopped by a threefold repetition of the opening theme hammered out in a harmonic version. This leads to the last subject and answer.

This movement is on a larger scale than the vocal ones analysed and is a typical ritornello concerto movement. The ritornellos are like great bastions holding the movement together in between which the solo group gives variety of sound though not of theme. The key is strong, tonic, dominant, relative minor, subdominant, tonic. The solo sections are interesting. B employs the three soloists, C the violin alone, D the flutes alone. The description fails to convey any of the essential musical quality. The movement in one of Bach's gayest and a chapter would be necessary to comment on its contrapuntal texture. One of the highlights is the fine swirl of sound when the violin is playing the semi-quaver passages at a quick two beats in the bar.

Church Cantata No. 11 Lobet Gott in seinen Reichen (Praise our God who reigns in Heaven) First movement Key D.

The next example is of an extended movement for choir and orchestra and again is typical of the large-scale plan of a Bach choral movement. Since the reader may not have a copy (more's the pity) the main themes are quoted.

The orchestra is the usual strings, flutes, oboes, three trumpets, and drums.

A¹ Bars 1–32 Orchestra alone	The opening ritornello is in binary form. a, b, and c of Ex. 41 are the three figures on which much of the movement is built. From the tonic key of D it modulates to A at bar 16 then through B minor, E minor and back to D.
B Bars 33–72 Chorus and orchestra	The chorus enters with a new theme (Ex. 42) but quickly makes use of the opening three figures. Much of the orchestral material has al-

ready been heard but the chorus superimposes its own vocal lines. For instance bars 1–16 are repeated at bars 41–56. The modulation is towards A major ending with a perfect cadence at bar 72.

A² Bars 73–88 Ritornello in A major.
Orchestra

C Bars 89–104 The chorus has a new syncopated theme (Ex. 43)
Chorus and starting in A major but modulating via
orchestra F sharp minor to B minor and ending with a strong cadence in that key.

Bach, Cantata No. 11 'Lobet Gott' (*Praise our God*)
1st movement, bars 1–4

A3 Bars 105–120   Ritornello in B minor. The four bars of the
Chorus and   opening ritornello which were in B minor
orchestra   (bars 17–20) are made the starting point and
the next four bars (109–112) modulate to E
minor as did 21–24. Bar 120 has a cadence in
B minor.

D   Bars 121–137   The chorus uses the same figure as in Section C
Chorus and   and modulates through G major, E minor and
orchestra   ends in F sharp minor.

A4 Bars 138–141   Ritornello in tonic key. Four bars are now
Orchestra   enough to re-establish the key and main
theme.

B2 Bars 142–185   This is a recapitulation and the section 142–157
Chorus and   is the same as 33–48 and the end of the section
orchestra   transposes into the tonic key what was in the
dominant.

A5 Bars 186–208   Ritornello in tonic key. A repetition of bars
1–16 (Bach does not trouble to write this out
again but puts *Dal Segno al Fine*).

The movement is extraordinarily satisfying. Apart from the
character of the themes there is a gradual building of a firm
structure. The subtle differences of the ritornello when the chorus
takes over from the orchestra and the different tone-quality
maintain the interest; we are always listening to different facets
of the same material. The regular return of the ritornello
impresses it more and more on our minds and its last
appearance in the same simple form as the first satisfies our sense
of balance.

The formula is A1 B A2 C A3 D A4 B2 A5. There is
a definite feeling of recapitulation at A4 followed by B2 A5;
this section matches the opening A1 B A2 which ends in the
dominant.

The reader should now analyse other Bach movements so that
he may obtain a good grasp of ritornello form. Many books on
form fight shy of Bach and students are given little help over
analysing many works which they admire. They know that the
movements of the suite are mainly in binary form, but the form

of the more extended movements is a closed book.* Bach was the greatest master in organising fugue and it is reasonable to expect his powers of planning to be evident in other movements.

The ritornello form is perhaps not as straightforward to analyse as a sonata movement, but to imagine that there is no analysable form shows that either our conception of form is wrong or that we cannot trace the course of a theme.

The concerto movements not in ritornello form may use binary form or a dance movement. In his concerti grossi Handel uses amongst other dances, minuet, hornpipe, siciliana and musette. In slower movements Bach often uses an ostinato bass and above it writes a long elaborate melody (the second movements of the violin concertos in A minor and E major). The number of movements is not fixed; the majority of Bach's concertos have three movements, whereas Handel's concerti grossi range from four to seven.

The Classical Concerto

From the time of Mozart onward we find that the group of soloists gives way to the single performer. The concertante and ripieno of the earlier period are now called solo and tutti (literally 'all'). The form reached its peak in this period and while it retained the idea of the ritornello it incorporated elements of the sonata. This was only to be expected since the concerto and sonata developed side by side.

Mozart did for the concerto what Bach did for the cantata, he wrote so much in the form and the quality of his work was so high that he established himself as its chief architect.

The main feature of the earlier concerto is still kept and the interest still lies in the development of the opening tutti by soloist and orchestra. The tension caused by the two opposing forces is made even stronger because the opening tutti is now much longer. The soloist may play a short introductory phrase

* Stewart Macpherson in *Form in Music* dismisses the early concerto in a short paragraph and two footnotes. The only detailed piece of information he gives is inaccurate. 'His (Bach's) so-called "Italian" Concerto in F is a piece written for the clavichord and is more like a solo-sonata.' The work was written for a double keyboard harpsichord and the concerto effect is obtained by the contrast of the two manuals.

with the orchestra, but after that he is silent until the whole of the opening ritornello has been played. The ritornello centres round the tonic key, any modulation being incidental and not part of the plot. The entry of the soloist after the ritornello draws immediate attention to him, and this shifting of emphasis from orchestra to soloist and vice versa is all part of the concerto idiom. The orchestra often collaborates with the soloist, occasionally having important asides to make, but its main task is to support him and supply a background against which he can appear more clearly. He plays his own versions of the themes, generally adorning them with figures that are characteristic of the instrument and showing them in a new light. His version, too, shows the influence of the sonata, since somewhere will come the second subject-group. This may use some of the themes given out previously by the orchestra or may be something not previously heard. During the remainder of the movement the themes are developed and recapitulated. As in sonata form, the recapitulation presents the themes in the tonic key, generally stating all those heard both in the opening orchestral ritornello and in the soloist's version. The recapitulation reconciles the two forms; the soloist and orchestra are now together, whereas in the opening they were separated. Towards the end of the recapitulation the orchestra builds up to a climax and pauses on the second inversion of the tonic triad. This is the signal for the cadenza (see pp. 79 & 80) in which the soloist displays his talents as a musician and as a performer. The orchestra re-enters and the movement is brought to a close with a short coda.

Sometimes the concerto is said to have a 'double exposition'. If one disregards the evolution of the concerto and regards it as allied to the symphony, then the opening orchestral ritornello could be described as an imperfect exposition and the soloist's version the normal one.

The term is not a good description because the two expositions are normally dissimilar in thematic content. The 'second exposition' omits some themes of the 'first exposition' and often adds new ones. In some cases the opening theme of the second subject-group is missing in the 'first exposition'; this important omission shows the 'double exposition' theory to be misleading. Concerto form developed alongside sonata form, and although the two have many common features the myth of the double exposition* (long since exploded by Tovey) does not stand scrutiny.

The second movement of the classical concerto does not create the tension that the first does by its conflict of unequal masses. By now the forces have come to terms with each other and there would be no point in a long ritornello movement. As in the majority of three movement works, the middle is the most lyrical, although here again Mozart sometimes adheres to the ritornello form. Very often a species of ternary form or a simple extension of it is used; occasionally there is an air and variations. The orchestra and soloist share the melodies in a gentle duet and their subdued voices blend in happy equality.

Rondo form is the most usual for the last movement. The various melodic sections follow one another, and the melodies, as in the slow movement, are shared between tutti and solo, although again Mozart is sometimes more complex. A cadenza sometimes appears in this movement.

Two examples of classical concerto will be analysed, Mozart's Piano Concerto in B flat (K.450) and Beethoven's Violin Concerto in D, Op. 61.

Concerto in B flat (K.450), Mozart

First movement Allegro

Bars 1–60   The orchestral ritornello uses four main themes, the openings of which are shown. The first, bars 1–14 (Ex. 44), the second, bars 14–25 (Ex. 45), the third, bars 26–41 (Ex. 46), the fourth, bars 42–53 (Ex. 47) with cadential phrases 53–60. There are ten perfect cadences in the tonic key apart from many half cadences and inverted cadences.

* It is true that the double-exposition theory fits Mozart's A major Clavier Concerto (K. 488) and Beethoven's Concerto for Pianoforte in C minor, but they are the exception for the classical period.

59–137   The soloist enters with a running figure while the orchestra is finishing its tutti and continues with it until a pause at bar 70. The soloist then states the opening theme very lightly accompanied. At bar 87 there is a new theme in G minor (Ex. 48) which eventually moves in semiquavers, and at bar 104 the second subject is announced (Ex. 49). The soloist has the first half and the orchestra the second. Another theme follows (Ex. 50) which alternates between tonic and dominant, leading into the closing section with the usual Mozart trill preceded by a chromatic scale (bars 135–136).

137–154   The orchestra quotes in the dominant two sections previously heard in the tonic (137–140 from 14–17 and 141–154 from 45–58).

155–196   The soloist begins an episode, later assisted by the orchestra. This cannot be regarded as a development section since the material is quite new.

197–308   The recapitulation of the first theme, bars 197–210, and the second theme, bars 210–214, the ending of which is changed to allow the soloist to recapitulate an altered version of the G minor theme (Ex. 48) which now appears in C minor. This leads the way to the second subject proper now in the key of the tonic, bars 232–247. The orchestra and soloist together have the theme which has not been used since its first appearance in bars 26–41. Bars 264–284 are the transposed form with some alterations of bars 119–137. The orchestra has a transposed version of bars 41–48 which leads to the cadenza. Mozart's cadenza extends the material just played by the orchestra and incorporates some of the earlier themes. At its close the orchestra in bars 295–308 has the tonic version of 49–59, the extra

bars being a succession of cadence chords as a
short coda.

Ex.44 Mozart, Piano Concerto in B flat (K.450)
Allegro 1st movement, bars 1–2

Ex.45 the same
bars 25–27

Ex.46 the same
bars 14–15

Ex.47 the same
bars 45–46

Ex.48 the same
bars 87–90

Ex.49 the same
bars 104–105

Ex.50 the same
bars 119–120

Of the four themes in the opening ritornello only one is used by the soloist. He has at least three themes which do not appear in the ritornello, including the main second subject. There is no development section, but instead, a middle episode. The recapitulation uses all the seven themes played earlier, some of which had not been heard since the opening ritornello.

Second movement Air with variations (Andante) Key E flat

For a general description of the form see Chapter Fourteen. The theme is a simple sixteen-bar melody, but as the soloist repeats each half after the orchestra it takes thirty-two bars. The same repetition occurs in the two variations, but the soloist plays throughout and the orchestra occasionally leaves him unaccompanied. The last part of the last variation is extended to form a coda.

Third movement Rondo-sonata (Allegro) Key B flat

A¹ Bars	1–76	The opening rondo theme in $\frac{6}{8}$ time is a
A(i)	1–16	simple eight-bar phrase containing two sequential repetitions of a two-bar motif and a two-bar cadential phrase played by the soloist and repeated by the orchestra (Ex. 51).
A(ii)	17–22	A second theme in the tonic on the
A(iii)	23–42	orchestra (Ex. 52) followed by a third
A(iv)	43–74	(Ex. 53) leading the way to an eight-bar theme (Ex. 54) still in the tonic, given out by the soloist and repeated and extended by the orchestra.
	75–76	A two-bar link leads straight into a
B¹	77–112	theme in the dominant moving in quavers,
B(i)	77–92	which is repeated and extended (Ex. 55).
B(ii)	93–112	A second dominant theme on a pedal F (Ex. 56). Although its first note is E flat, the four-bar phrase on which it is built holds to the key of F. After 16 bars the pedal F becomes the dominant of B flat leading the way to A².

A²	113–141	A return of the main rondo theme by the piano and extended when the orchestra repeats it, leading to eight bars on the dominant of G minor in which key we would expect an episode. However, a dominant seventh in E flat for two bars leads to
C	141–168	An episode in E flat major (Ex. 57).
Development	168–210	This begins in E flat with the main rondo theme. The drop of a sixth in its second bar (Ex. 51) now becomes a seventh.
A³	210–240	The rondo theme in the tonic. There are now thirty-one bars instead of the former seventy-six, themes Aii, iii and iv being omitted.
B²	240–284	The second subject-group where Bi and Bii are in the tonic.
	284	The cadenza. Themes Ai, in both its forms (with a drop of a sixth and a seventh) and C are used.
A⁴	285–316	Final entry of main rondo theme Aii, which had not been heard since its first appearance, is extended to make a coda on the tonic pedal.

Ex. 51

Allegro   3rd movement, bars 1–8

Ex. 52

                                                    the same
                                                    bars 16–20

This movement shows itself as a real sonata-rondo and may be summarised as:

A¹ B A² C (episode and development) A³ B Cadenza A⁴. There are seven main themes, four in the tonic key, two in the dominant and an episodical theme in the subdominant. We are provided with both an episode and a development, and the cadenza carries the development still further. The interesting use of Aii, which was reserved to the end, is a master touch and gives the movement unity. Themes Aiii and iv are only heard in the exposition. Aiii is not very significant, but few composers could afford to let Aiv blossom once only.

Concerto for Violin and Orchestra in D major. Op. 61 Beethoven

First movement Allegro ma non troppo

There are six themes heard during the orchestral ritornello (bars 1–101) numbered i–vi in the following analysis. They cannot be classified into first or second subject-groups until the solo entry defines their keys. The soloist enters at the cadence point of the orchestral ritornello which is extended from bar 89–101. In this movement the soloist plays the second subject-group twice, making with the orchestral ritornello a three-fold statement of these themes.

Bars   1–18 (i) The opening subject introduced by a bar of tonic drum-taps (Ex. 58).

      18–27 (ii) A scalic theme in tonic (Ex. 59).

      28–35 (iii) A fortissimo chordal theme in B flat (Ex. 60).

      35–42 (iv) A vigorous semiquaver movement on tonic and dominant chords in D minor (Ex. 61). The latter chord is also the dominant of D major in which key the next theme comes.

A   43–77 (v) A flowing theme built on a two-bar motif in key D (Ex. 62) then played in tonic minor.

      77–101(vi) A theme divided between treble and bass in tonic (Ex. 63). During this the solo violin enters and the hierarchy of the themes is made clear by the keys employed.

      102–118 First subject in tonic (i) above.

      118–143 Transition (ii) above. Theme is extended and leads to the second subject-group.

      144–223 (v) (vi) above, now in dominant key.

      224–238 A second transition on (iii) and (iv) above leading to

      239–283 A restatement of the second subject-group (v and vi). Although (v) is still in dominant (vi) is now in C major.

      284–365 Development.

      365–382 First subject in tonic

      382–417 Transition on (ii) lengthened

      418–497 Second subject-group (v and vi) in tonic

      497–510 Themes (iii) and (iv) do not lead as before to a repetition of (v) and (vi) but into the cadenza.

      511–535 A coda on the opening theme.

Beethoven, Violin Concerto in D major Op. 61
1st movement, bars 1–5

Second movement Larghetto in G major

The key never really changes in this movement which has two themes. The first (Ex. 64) is used as the basis for variations and the second (Ex. 65) provides diversity.

A¹ Bars 1–40   Three variations on the first theme of ten bars.

40–44   A link passage in the form of a small cadenza leading to

B¹   45–52   Second theme in tonic.

53–55   A short link leading to

A²	55–71	First theme repeated with a short extension on a tonic pedal.
B²	71–79	Second theme.
	80–88	The theme used at bar 65 links on to a repetition of the first two bars of A¹.

Three bars and a 'cadenza ad lib' lead without break into the last movement.

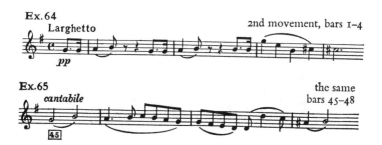

Ex. 64
Larghetto
2nd movement, bars 1–4
pp

Ex. 65
cantabile
the same
bars 45–48
45

Third Movement Rondo in Key D

| A¹ | Bars 1–45 | The main theme (Ex. 66) is given out by the soloist and then by the orchestra. In the orchestral section a complementary theme is added (Ex. 67). |

Transition

	45–48	Another gay theme is introduced (Ex. 68).
B¹	59–92	First episode (or second subject) in dominant (Ex. 69).
A²	92–126	Repeat of main rondo theme in tonic.
C	127–173	Second episode in G minor (Ex. 70) with a secondary section beginning at bar 143.
A³	174–218	Repeat of main rondo theme in tonic (same as bars 1–45).

Transition

| | 219–232 | Begins as before, but now altered to lead into the tonic key instead of the dominant. |

B²   233–268   First episode (or second subject) in tonic,
                leading the way to a tutti.
      268–278   Tutti built on transitional theme. (Ex. 68).

Cadenza

Coda   279–359 A long coda built on the opening rondo theme.
                Its length is evidence of its importance in the
                structural scheme. (Bar 340 has an interesting
                rhythmical feature more characteristic of
                Brahms than Beethoven.) (Ex. 71.)

Ex. 66   3rd movement, bars 1–4

                                                    the same
Ex. 67   bars 31–32

                                                    the same
Ex. 68   bars 46–47

                                                    the same
Ex. 69   bars 59–60

                                                    the same
Ex. 70   bars 127–130

                                                    the same
                                                    bars 340–342
Ex. 71

This movement is a typical Beethoven rondo-sonata movement, and the differences between it and the last movement of Mozart's concerto (analysed previously) should be noted.

Later development

During the course of the nineteenth century the gradual departure from the ideal form of Mozart became more noticeable. The chief difference is that of the treatment of the first movement. Mozart's ritornello movement is replaced by one in normal sonata form. This is not true of the concertos of Brahms who does not always discard the opening ritornello, but the general attitude of the romantic composers is to let the soloist and the orchestra share the exposition from its beginning. For instance, in the Mendelssohn violin concerto the soloist opens with the first subject and in the Schumann piano concerto the soloist repeats the first subject immediately after it has been stated by the orchestra. The tension formerly created by the long orchestral ritornello vanishes and the two forces are accepted as equal partners. Romanticism, too, brought a new interest in orchestral colour and composers explored the variety of sounds obtained by a combination of solo instrument and orchestra. All the changes that affected musical composition naturally affected the concerto. A feeling for a more rhapsodic style is evident and there is a less rigid attitude to musical form. For example, the second piano concerto of Liszt is in one movement and the composer tries further to unify it by means of thematic metamorphosis (a new theme is made by varying the note-lengths of an earlier one). Dvořák used his native dances, the Furiant and the Dumka, in his 'cello concerto in B minor. The linking of the concerto with the variation is shown in such works as the 'Symphonic Variations' of César Franck and the 'Totentanz' of Liszt.

However, the cadenza has remained a feature of the concerto and its importance justifies more detailed comment.

The instrumental cadenza had its origin in the ornamentation of the cadence of the aria. It was the custom for the singer to improvise at the cadence. He was given an opportunity to display his technique and also to add to the effectiveness of the aria by inserting on the spur of the moment a phrase which would clinch the musical argument. At least that is what might have happened occasionally in the most effective cadenzas. But the cadenza became more and more a place where the singer could exhibit outstanding feats of vocalisation. Some composers, used as they were to the customs of their day, must always have had qualms when certain performers arrived at the cadence. Also its improvisatory nature would tend to lose its freshness. A singer would find a convenient phrase and, as with improvisation all down the ages, the same path would be taken until it became a well-worn rut.

There is more scope for improvisation when harmony as well as melody is involved, and in the hands of a Bach, a Handel or a Mozart, a cadenza must have been a thrilling affair. Even in less inspired hands it was probably very effective since improvisation was one of the normal techniques of the eighteenth-century musician. In the early eighteenth century the cadenza was a responsibility of the performer, but Mozart and Beethoven often wrote it out in full. This practice became customary in the nineteenth century.

What of those eighteenth-century concertos, especially those of Mozart, which are not provided with a cadenza by the composer? Musical decency should ensure that the cadenza should be in the same style as the concerto. A cadenza in nineteenth-century style does not fit an eighteenth-century concerto, but unfortunately this mixture of styles is often heard on the concert platform. In the same way as an architect has to give life to an antique style when rebuilding a house in a Georgian crescent, so a musician has to be able to compose a cadenza in eighteenth-century style to fit a concerto of similar date. Mozart has provided many guides in the cadenzas he has written. He realised that the musical interest must be sustained but not to the extent of making the cadenza a second development. He was a conserver of notes and was able to hold the balance between musical interest and technical display.

CHAPTER NINE

The Overture

Originally an overture was a musical introduction to an opera. It was necessary to have some indication that the opera was about to begin and the obvious way would to be let the orchestra play loudly. This description applies to the opening bars of Monteverdi's opera *Orfeo* (1607). There are eight bars of a toccata-like flourish on the chord of C major played by all the instruments with the trumpet very much in evidence. This is followed by a ritornello of eight bars which is repeated five times: in between each repetition the Spirit of Music sings the prologue, and her last words ask the audience to be quiet. The curtain then rises on the first act. This introduction was called the 'Sinfonia avanti l'opera' (the symphony before the opera). But it was not until the time of Alessandro Scarlatti (1659–1725) and Lully (1633–87) that the overture began to be a movement of importance. Their names are associated with the Italian overture and the French overture respectively. Not that these forms sprang fully fledged into existence; there are earlier examples,* but these men repeatedly used the forms.

The Italian overture has three sections: the first a quick movement, sometimes fugal, using the full band; the second a slow movement more lightly orchestrated, and the last a quick movement, generally in binary form, of the gay presto type in which the full band again takes part.

The French overture also has three sections: the first slow and pompous in which the dotted rhythm $\frac{4}{4}$ ♩. ♪ ♩. ♪ etc. prevails. This section was repeated. The second a fugal allegro (sometimes repeated) and the third either a return to the slow

---

* HAM 208 is a Sinfonia by Landi (*c.* 1590–*c.* 1653) showing the Italian form and HAM 223 an overture by Cambert (1628?–1677) showing the French form.

tempo of the first section or a dance, often a minuet. The overture was often followed by a series of dance movements.

The Italian overture is one of the many Italian forms which are regarded as the forerunners of the symphony. The French overture became more established in its own right and better known since it was used by Purcell, Handel and Bach amongst others. Purcell's overture to the *Indian Queen* (1664) is a French overture having a slow introduction with the dotted-note figure, a fugal allegro and a short final adagio. His overture to *Dido and Aeneas* shows the same form with the omission of the final adagio. Handel's overture to *Samson* has the three sections, the last being a minuet. The *Messiah* overture has the opening two sections and a return to the slow tempo of the opening for a few bars, just long enough to provide the final climax. Bach made much use of the form, he even used it as the opening chorus of some of the church cantatas. In Cantata 61 'Nun Komm der Heiden Heiland' (*Come, Redeemer*) the first movement is headed 'Ouverture' and against the dotted-note figures of the strings he puts the opening two lines of the chorale. This is neatly contrived, each voice sings the first line in turn, the second line being in four-part harmony. The writing is so skilful that the orchestral part sounds complete in itself, a typical opening adagio. The third line is treated fugally in four parts at a quicker tempo, the strings doubling the voices, and the fourth line comes back to the opening adagio with a fine climax in the orchestra after the voices have finished. Bach used the form in more orthodox ways in the fourth Partita and in variation 16 of the 'Goldberg' Variations.

In the French opera the opening movements of the overture were followed by dances, so in the collection of dances called a suite (see chapter ten), the first movement was often an overture. Bach calls his four orchestral suites 'Ouvertures'.

The overture of the opera or oratorio was a self-contained work and was not generally specifically connected, thematically or emotionally, with the music that followed. The reforms of Gluck improved the dramatic effect of the overture, since he lets the overture (with the exception of *Orfeo*) prepare the mind of the audience for the drama that was to follow.

Mozart's overtures are cast in sonata form, often with a slow introduction and without the repeat of the exposition that was customary in the symphony. Sometimes in place of the development section there is an episode, but an important feature of the Mozart overture is the use of themes that are later to be heard in the opera (*Don Giovanni*, *Magic Flute*). The same happens in Beethoven's *Fidelio* overtures and in the overtures of Weber. There were also overtures to plays which of necessity were independent orchestral pieces. Such are the overtures to *Egmont*, *Coriolan* (Beethoven) and *A Midsummer Night's Dream* (Mendelssohn).

An offshoot of the operatic overture was the concert overture, which was usually in sonata form. The composer was writing neither for the opera nor for the theatre and he could let the work portray whatever mood he chose. It was a self-contained piece of music and the title would indicate the origin of the work which was often literary. Three examples of concert overtures are Mendelssohn's *Hebrides*, Berlioz's *Le Carnaval Romain* and Brahms's *Tragic*.

During the nineteenth century the operatic overture became less important in itself but was used more and more to prepare the way for the opera. Wagner wrote independent overtures to *Rienzi*, *The Flying Dutchman* and *Tannhäuser*, but from *Lohengrin* onwards we find he often uses the word Vorspiel for the music preceding the rise of the curtain. In each there is no break before the first scene once the orchestra has begun. *Parsifal* and *Meistersinger* have long and interesting overtures but they both lead naturally into the opera. A concert version of *Meistersinger* misses the climax of the opera house—the rise of the curtain on the scene in St. Katherine's Church.

CHAPTER TEN

The Suite

A suite is a collection of two or more pieces, generally contrasted. The content of the suite varies according to the period, but the word generally refers either to the classical suite (approximately 1650–1750) or to the modern suite of the nineteenth and twentieth centuries.

Before the period of the classical suite the grouping of two contrasting dances, one slow and one fast, gave variety. Sometimes a common theme linked them. Many sixteenth-century Italian publications for lute illustrate this and later, when music was published for the early keyboard instruments, the same grouping was followed. In 'Parthenia or The Maydenhead of the first musicke that euer was printed for the Virginnalls' (1611), there are many pavans and galliards, and in the 'Fitzwilliam Virginal Book' there are examples of two dances grouped together. When the fashion in dances changed, the allemande and courante replaced the pavan and the galliard. Collections of instrumental pieces tended to be based on this slow-fast relationship. By the time of Bach and Handel the group of dances known as a suite contained generally at least two pairs of alternating movements slow-fast-slow-fast. No longer, however, were they used for dancing, and movements of a different type were often inserted.

Although in England and France the word 'suite' was generally used, in England the word would often be 'lesson' and in France 'ordre'. The word 'partita'* was used by Bach and others and the Italian equivalent was the 'sonata da camera'. Whatever name was given to the collection of movements, the contents were almost entirely of dance tunes written for keyboard or for an

---

* For another meaning of this word see Chapter Fourteen, p.141.

instrumental group. The contents of suites by Purcell, Couperin, Corelli, Bach and Handel are given below and the dances are described in detail later.

Purcell

The eight suites of Purcell are fairly consistent both in the number and type of movements. All have four movements except Nos. 3, 6 and 7, which have three. In the four-movement suites the order is prelude, almand and courante, but the fourth dance varies. It is a minuet in Suites 1 and 8; a sarabande in Suites 2 and 4. Suite No. 3 has prelude, almand and courante, and No. 6 prelude, almand, hornpipe, and No. 7, almand, courante, hornpipe.

In the 'Second Part of Musick's Handmaid', and 'A Choice Collection of Lessons' there are movements headed Chaconne, Rigadoon, March, Jig and Cibell (or Trumpet Tune).

Couperin

The First Suite in G minor has 18 movements, four of which have merely the name of the dance, four have the dance name preceded by a title and the remainder just the title. Although in some cases the latter are in dance form such as the tenth movement (*La Nanette*), which is like a bourrée, in the main they cannot be classified as dances. They are short descriptive pieces with sometimes amusing titles 'Les Plaisirs de St. Germain-en-Laye' and 'Les Nonètes' (*The Young Nuns*) divided into two sections 'Les Blondes' and 'Les Brunes', Couperin distinguishes these two female species by a change of mode. This change of mode is moderately frequent in Couperin. Three of the movements are in rondo form (ABACA) and are so described by the composer, 'Les Silvains' (*Forest Gods*)—Rondeau; 'Les Abeilles' (*The Bees*)—Rondeau; and 'L'Enchanteresse' (*The Enchantress*)—Rondeau. Couperin seems to have grown less interested in the dance forms since they certainly occur less in his later suites. His four books of harpsichord music contain 27 suites with 230 pieces. Many are miniature tone-poems, delicate and tasteful, and have a clarity of expression typical of French art.

Corelli

The six Sonate da Camera Op. 4 each begin with a preludio which may be a movement in binary form as in Sonata No. 3 or merely six bars of slow introduction as in No. 6. Of the dances, the corrente is the most used and appears in five of the sonatas. The allemanda* appears four times, the giga and the gavotta twice and the sarabanda once. Some of the movements are not in dance forms and have only the Italian words Adagio or Allegro as the heading. Occasionally the key is changed to the dominant for one of the movements as in Sonata No. 2.

Bach

Each of the 18 keyboard suites of Bach (six English Suites, six French Suites and six Partitas) has six or more movements. The Partitas each begin with a different movement, prelude, sinfonia, fantasia, ouverture, prèambule and toccata. Each has an allemande, a courante, a sarabande and a gigue except the second which omits the gigue. The allemande and courante invariably follow the opening movement; sometimes another movement comes before the sarabande (No. 4 aria, No. 5 air) and one or more movements come before the last. These movements are, in No. 1, minuet; in No. 2, rondeau and this ends with a caprice; in No. 3 burlesca and scherzo; in No. 4 menuet; in No. 5 tempo di menuetto and passepied; in No. 6 tempo di gavotta. The English Suites each begin with a prelude followed by allemande, courante, sarabande, and end with a gigue. The preludes, except for the first, are long imposing movements in concerto form. There is a pair of dances between the sarabande and the gigue; in Nos. 1 and 2, two bourrées; in Nos. 3 and 6, two gavottes; in No. 4, two minuets, and in No. 5, two passepieds.

The French Suites each begin with an allemande, courante and sarabande, and end with a gigue, but as in the English Suites there are other dances between the sarabande and gigue. No. 1 has two menuets; No. 2, an air and a menuet; No. 3, an

---

* The Italian spelling of 'Allemande'. The names of the common dances have become anglicised and these have been used in the text except when a particular composition is mentioned. Bach, for instance, generally uses the French titles.

anglaise and two menuets; No. 4, a gavotte, a menuet and an air; No. 5, a gavotte, a bourrée and a loure; No. 6, a gavotte, a polonaise, a bourrée and a menuet.

Handel

In the first eight suites of Handel the allemande appears four times, the courante four times, the sarabande twice and the gigue five times. He begins five with a prelude, one with an ouverture (the French form), one with an adagio, and one with a fugue. The fugue also makes its appearance in suites No. 2, 3, 6, and 8. Several movements merely have andante, allegro, etc. as headings and there are two sets of airs and variations and a passacaglia. It will be noticed that Handel does not rely entirely on dance movements but writes more in the Italian sonata style.

The above lists represent some of the keyboard works of five well-known composers of the period. But it should be evident that there was great variety in the suite and that to think of it always as allemande, courante, sarabande and gigue with a one or two optional 'extras' is not a correct interpretation of the facts. The idea has probably arisen through the French suites of Bach; these are the easiest of Bach's to play and so probably better known and they conform to the popular definition. Another factor to take into account is the scale of the movements. Although in the French suites the movements are in scale with each other, in the English suites (except No. 1) the first movement overshadows the rest. These great preludes, close-knit and intense in expression, make the dances that follow seem almost lightweight. They have the same relationship to the prelude as the dances that followed the French overtures of Lully.

The key of the opening movement of the suite was normally kept throughout. Bach, like Couperin, occasionally puts a movement into the relative or tonic major or minor. In the Partitas and French suites there is no change at all, but in all the English suites there is one movement in the corresponding tonic major or minor, except for No. 4 which has a movement in the relative minor. Handel, like Corelli, prefers the relative major or minor to the tonic major or minor.

The dance movements are almost all in binary form. The minuet and gavotte are sometimes in ternary or incline towards it by the repetition of the opening bars at the end of the movement. Rondo form is used especially by the French composers Couperin and Rameau.

Bach in the English Suite No. 3 has passepied 1, 'en rondeau' in which the opening section appears twice later in the usual ABACA formula. Passepied II which follows is in binary form and then passepied I is repeated again, making a larger ternary structure. This larger ternary is frequently seen in the same way with minuets and gavottes. Bach in the third French Suite has menuet I, menuet II, followed by menuet I. The opening movement, when it was not a dance, was more free and might be a rhapsodic prelude, a French overture, a ritornello movement or indeed any type of movement.

In a suite the form and key of each movement rarely varies. The essential difference is in the mood of each dance or movement. There is variety in the number of beats in the bar, in the differing speeds and characteristic time patterns.

Short descriptions of the dances of the suite are given below:

Allemande. The suite form of the allemande is not really a dance.* It is in moderate $\frac{4}{4}$ time and flowing, tending to be contrapuntal and using semiquaver movement. A characteristic feature is its beginning on the last semiquaver of a bar or more rarely the last three semiquavers.

Courante (Fr.), *Coranto* or *Corrente* (It.). There are two kinds, the French and the Italian. The Italian is the quick running kind, true to its name, and in triple-time ($\frac{3}{4}$ or $\frac{3}{8}$). The French is slower and generally written in $\frac{3}{2}$ time. It was the popular dance at the court of Louis XIV and is more complex in movement than the simple Italian form. A prevalent rhythm is the ♩.♪ and at the cadences $\frac{3}{2}$ becomes $\frac{6}{4}$ and this change sometimes appears elsewhere. Couperin frequently used $\frac{6}{4}$ as the time-signature, but that does not preclude occasional $\frac{3}{2}$ bars. The dance begins on the

---

* 'The allemande still danced today amongst the peasants of Germany and Switzerland is a different thing; like the Ländler, it is prophetic of the waltz being in three-beats-in-a-measure and lively.' Scholes *Companion to Music*.

last part of the bar, generally the last quarter of the beat. It was sometimes followed by a more ornamented version called a 'double'.

Sarabande. A slow dance in triple time beginning on the first beat of the bar. Its rhythmical feature is the halt on the second beat occurring at the cadence and elsewhere, making a feminine ending. A typical pattern is $\frac{3}{2}$ ♩ ♩ . ♩|♩ ○ |. It is more harmonic than contrapuntal. Like the courante the sarabande may be followed by an ornamental version called a 'double'.

Gigue (Fr.), *Giga* (It.). There are two kinds, French and Italian. The French is a lively dance in which the division of the bar or beat is in three. $\frac{3}{8}$, $\frac{6}{8}$ or $\frac{12}{8}$ are the most usual signatures but others are also used. The rhythmic feature is usually the 'long short' (♩ ♪) or there may be continuous movement. Many are in fugal style with much imitation. Sometimes the second half of the gigue begins by inverting the opening half. The Italian type (Giga) is quicker and not fugal and, like the corrente, has quick running passages built on a simple chord foundation. Bach writes the French kind except for Partita No. 1 and English Suite No. 2, which are Italian. The origin of the word is thought to have come from the English jig which is found in English music of the sixteenth century.

Minuet. A dance in triple time of moderate tempo. Although its character changed later, at the period of the suite, it was a courtly dance. Unlike the other dances of the suite it was often in ternary form. The minuet, for instance, of Couperin's second suite has an eight bar first section with a cadence in the tonic; this is repeated exactly at the end of the second section, making a definite ternary structure. This does not apply to the Bach suites, although the menuet in Partita No. 4 and menuet II in English suite No. 4 come very near it. The minuet was generally followed by another, often called a trio (menuet II in the Bach suites) after which the first minuet was repeated again making the whole a ternary structure. The trio was so called because the custom was for the second minuet to be played not by the full band but by three instruments. The word trio came later to be used for the second minuet even when it was not in three parts.

The minuet and trio was the only dance to be carried over into the symphony.

The Gavotte. A moderately quick dance in $\frac{4}{4}$ or C time, generally beginning on the half-bar.* Gay in character and, like the minuet, sometimes in ternary form. The basic rhythm was not disturbed by being broken up into semiquavers, and most gavottes are sparing even of quavers. It was sometimes followed by another usually called a musette in which a drone bass prevailed. This was imitative of the French cornemuse (bagpipe). The first gavotte was then repeated making, like the minuet and trio, a ternary structure. The form was, therefore, either gavotte I, gavotte II, gavotte I, or gavotte I, musette, gavotte I. Some of the earlier gavottes begin on the first beat of the bar.

Bourrée (English *Borre*, *Borry*, etc.). A dance of the gavotte type but rather faster, beginning on the fourth beat of the bar. Like the gavotte it was often followed by a second dance after which the first was repeated.

Passepied (English *Paspy*). A lively dance usually in $\frac{3}{8}$ generally beginning on the third beat. Often followed by a second. In Bach's English suite No. 5 the second passepied is in tonic major; in Couperin's suite No. 2 the passepied is definitely in ternary form.

Dances which are less common are:

Loure. The best known example of this dance is in Bach's French suite No. 5. It was like a gigue but rather slower and its characteristic rhythm was the short accented first note and the longer unaccented second. The time-signature was usually $\frac{6}{4}$.

Polonaise. A graceful and stately dance in triple time originating from Poland. The rhythmic feature is the cadence on the weak part of the bar, usually the second beat. This beat is made important in the rhythmic figures which are often repeated in successive bars. The same figure is often kept within the bar (♫♩♫♩♫♩). The several polonaises in the Anna Magdalena Bach Book should be examined. The latter version of the dance by Chopin, Weber, Liszt, etc., uses similar rhythms, but because of the romantic idiom

---

* In *Form in Music* Macpherson says 'beginning always at the half-bar', but there are very many examples that begin differently.

the musical effect is quite different. The basic polonaise rhythm is generally given to the left hand accompaniment, and the right hand accentuates it by its melody.

Hornpipe. An English dance used by Purcell, and occasionally by Handel. Generally in $\frac{3}{2}$ time with the cadence on the third beat, quite different from the later two-in-a-bar sailor's dance. Examples can be found in Purcell's suites No. 6 and 7.

Rigaudon (English *Rigadoon*). A dance, somewhat like the bourrée in duple or quadruple time, usually beginning on the last part of the bar. However, a Rigadoon by Purcell in 'The Second Part of Musick's Hand-maid' begins on the first beat.

Chaconne and Passacaglia. These two dances were of similar nature, being in slow triple time. The interesting feature was that the dances were built on a ground bass, usually an eight bar phrase with one chord in each bar. Since this provided an easy way of extending a composition it was applied to other pieces as well. The chaconne and passacaglia are dealt with in more detail in chapter fourteen.

Siciliano. A seventeenth/eighteenth-century dance in a slow $\frac{6}{8}$ or $\frac{12}{8}$ time originating from Sicily. Pastoral in character and using the rhythmic figure ♪♫ which gives a swaying motion.

The Modern Suite

The name suite is used to describe a number of pieces grouped together by the composer. The pieces are generally short, not necessarily dances and often they are an arrangement of ballet or stage works. Grieg's *Peer Gynt* Suites are collections of the pieces he wrote for the production of the play of the same name by Ibsen. Stravinsky's *L'Oiseau de Feu* Suite is an arrangement for concert purposes of the ballet. Composers have sometimes imitated the early suite, e.g. *Tombeau de Couperin* by Ravel.

CHAPTER ELEVEN

The Early Sonata

The description of the sonata and of sonata form in Chapter Five applies to the later sonata which was composed from about 1750 onwards. This chapter will deal with the sonata in the preceding period.

In the latter part of the seventeenth and early part of the eighteenth centuries a sonata was described as sonata da camera or sonata da chiesa, i.e. chamber sonata or church sonata. The sonata da camera was a collection of dance movements described in the previous chapter. The sonata da chiesa was a more serious collection of movements suitable to be performed in church. Although on the face of it this may seem a sufficient line of demarcation, a moment's thought will show the difficulty of dividing instrumental music into that which is suitable for a chamber and that suitable for a church. Slow music is apt to be serious and fast music gay, be its title sonata da camera or sonata da chiesa. It would be difficult to decide the provenance of a movement unless it showed one of the characteristic dance rhythms and even then one could be mistaken, since Corelli, for instance, in his Sonata da Chiesa Op. 5, No. 3 ends with a gigue. So the two types were not always as distinctive as one would imagine. The sonata da chiesa was written for strings with a figured bass continuo, or for violin and orchestra with continuo, or for two violins and bass. The sonata for two violins and bass was also known as a sonata à tre (trio-sonata). Although there were only three lines of music, four players would be necessary because a chordal instrument (harpsichord, organ or lute), would supply the harmonies indicated by figures below the bass line.

The number of movements in these early sonatas was usually four; a slow introduction, a fugal movement, a slow one and a quick finale. As in the sonata da camera the key remained the same for each movement with an occasional change to the relative or tonic major or minor.

The form of the individual movement was varied and included binary, ternary, rondo and fugue or more commonly, a fugal allegro in ritornello form or in a ternary shape. Dance movements were used but they may or may not be specifically named. In addition the slow movements may be just a development of an opening phrase and not be long enough to require a binary or ternary structure. The slow movement also might be a development of a basso ostinato, the same bass phrase being repeated in various keys and on varying degrees of the scale, so holding the music together whilst the melody pursued its own line of development.

The early sonata is generally passed over quickly in most general books on form because it is often difficult to name the forms. The present writer does not go very much further but an attempt has been made to give short descriptions of sets of sonatas by well-known composers. The reader will then have some evidence of the methods of these composers and also he will have a starting point for his own investigations. It must be emphasised that any conclusions reached apply only to the works mentioned. This method has been chosen because it is difficult to generalise: it is far better to study specific works.

Although it might be difficult to examine early printed editions of eighteenth-century sonatas as they are found only in important libraries, many have now been reprinted in a modern performing edition.★

(1)	G. B. Vitali (c. 1644–92)	Sonata for 2 violins and continuo.
(2)	Corelli (1653–1713)	Sonatas Op. 5, 1–6 for violin and clavier.
(3)	Tartini (1692–1770)	12 Trio Sonatas Op. 3.
(4)	Handel (1685–1759)	6 Sonatas for 2 violins, 2 hautboys or German flutes Op. 2.
(5)	Boyce (1710–1779)	12 Sonatas for 2 violins with continuo.

★ Of those mentioned the Corelli, Handel and Bach are all available, but only selected sonatas for the remainder.

(6) Locatelli (1695–1764)   6 Sonatas for 2 German flutes or
                              2 violins with continuo Op. 3.

(7) Bach (1685–1750)   6 Sonatas for flute and clavier,
                              6 Sonatas for violin and clavier,
                              Sonatas 1, 3, and 5 for unaccom-
                              panied violin (the even numbered
                              sonatas are suites).
                              3 Sonatas for gamba and clavier,
                              the Trio from the Musical Offering.
                              This comprises all the Bach sonatas
                              except for those known as the
                              Organ Sonatas which are in a
                              different category.

*G. B. Vitali Sonata for two violins and continuo

Key A minor. Four movements.

The whole takes under five minutes to play. There seems little point in the second vivace unless it was meant as an easier alternative to the first; it is rather more harmonic whereas the first is contrapuntal.

1. *Vivace*   27 bars of $\frac{4}{4}$ time

    This is in binary form but instead of each section being repeated the whole movement is repeated, so that the two violins can interchange parts. The opening theme is quoted below.

Ex.72   Vitali, Sonata for two violins and continuo
Vn.I Vivace   1st movement, bars 1–5

There is variation on the repeat; an interrupted cadence marks its beginning and a short coda closes it. The first part

* HAM 245.

ends with a cadence in the tonic and the second section is an imitation of the first in the key of the dominant, but works back to the tonic for the last two bars.

2. *Vivace*   7 bars of $\frac{4}{4}$ time

The time pattern is the same as the opening vivace but the notes are different. There is little rhythmical development, but variety (all that is necessary in seven bars) is obtained by using the last figure of bar 3 Ex. 72.

3. *Largo*   27 bars of $\frac{3}{4}$ time

The characteristic halt on the second beat of the bar likens it to a sarabande. The whole divides into four phrases of six bars, the last being extended to a coda with the broadening effect of two bars of $\frac{3}{4}$ becoming one of $\frac{3}{2}$ (a common example of this is in bars 37 and 38 of 'And the glory of the Lord' from *Messiah*). The movement begins with a six-bar melody for the first violin repeated exactly in the dominant by the second violin. Both are together at the third phrase which begins with the rhythm of the opening two bars and works on that to the end.

4. *Vivace*   21 bars of $\frac{4}{4}$ time

The interesting point is that the movement begins in C major but at the sixth bar is back in A minor. These two keys appear to be equally important but A minor wins with the final cadence. The opening phrase in key C has three different patterns, the last being used later. The movement makes most use of the phrase introduced in A minor at bar 7. It reappears at bar 11 in C major and bar 15 in A minor.

G. B. Vitali 'was one of the first to distinguish clearly between the sonata da chiesa and the sonata da camera'.* This is an early example and the form reached its height in the first half of the eighteenth century, and some examples from later composers are given below.

As time went on the words 'da chiesa' and 'da camera' were no longer used, the later composers naming the collection of dances suites and the more serious works sonatas.

* HAM Vol. ii, p. 286.

Corelli Sonatas Op. 5, 1–6 for violin and clavier

There are 12 sonatas under this opus number. Nos. 1–6 being 'chiesa' and Nos. 7–12 'camera'. The former are described below. Each of the sonatas has five movements, two slow and three fast. Each has one movement in the relative major or minor. The individual forms vary but there are examples of binary form, fugal allegro and lyrical adagio in which one theme is developed. A brief analysis of Sonata No. 6 in A major is given.

1. *Grave*   27 bars of $\frac{4}{4}$ time

Although the movement has no double bar and repeat marks, it arrives at a perfect cadence in Key E about halfway through at bar 12. This first section divides up into three phrases of four bars containing the main ideas.

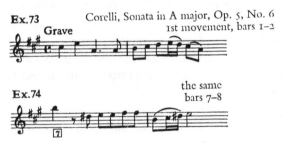

Ex.73   Corelli, Sonata in A major, Op. 5, No. 6
   Grave   1st movement, bars 1–2

Ex.74   the same
                                     bars 7–8

The second section touches B major and returns to the tonic via E major. Another idea is introduced at bar 16, and the section has two phrases of three bars and one of four followed by a five-bar coda on the last part of the opening theme.

2. *Allegro*   58 bars of $\frac{4}{4}$ time

Ex.75   2nd movement, bars 1–2
   Allegro

The subject of this fugal movement has already been foreshadowed in the adagio (Ex. 74). The fugal subject ends differently from the adagio but there is an exact appearance later in the movement. It appears alone on the violin and by means of double stopping an attempt is made at an answer. It then appears in the left hand of the clavier and eventually reaches a perfect cadence in the tonic at bar 19. It begins again in the same key, but a new theme is taken in modulating sequences and develops into an arpeggio 'moto perpetuo' figure. At bar 46 the subject returns and is used to the end except for an adagio coda.

3. *Allegro*   30 bars of $\frac{4}{4}$ time

An example of a 'moto perpetuo' movement so often found in Corelli. The harmony is very clear and the left hand of the clavier punctuates the phrases and defines the modulations. A perfect cadence in the tonic bar 5, in the dominant bar 10, in the submediant minor bar 16, in the tonic bar 22 and again in the final cadence. These cadences indicate the phrase-structure.

4. *Adagio in F sharp minor*   35 bars of $\frac{3}{2}$ time

A lyrical adagio in which the theme gradually develops. The falling interval, often a fifth, provides the characteristic motive. The phrases are varied in length, the cadences coming at bar 9 (tonic), 16 (relative major), 22 (subdominant minor), 33 (tonic), followed by two bars of coda. The opening phrase

Ex.76

Adagio   4th movement, bars 1–4

resembles the opening of the first movement.

5. *Allegro*   74 bars of $\frac{6}{8}$ time

The violin states the subject and by means of double stopping continues with the answer. The clavier has its share also and the first section, which keeps strictly to tonic and dominant, comes to a perfect cadence in the tonic at bar 28. An episode (a 'moto perpetuo' figure) leads to the subject in the relative minor at bar 36 with an answer a fifth higher. Another episode from bar 44 to 56 leads to the return of the theme in the tonic and the dominant. So this movement could be shown by the formula ABACA.

The same themes are often used in more than one movement. This applies to other sonatas in the same set and was, in fact, a far more common occurrence than is generally realised.

Handel Six Sonatas Op. 2 for two violins and bass

Each sonata has four movements except No. 4 which has five, and each follows the slow-quick-slow-quick pattern, the extra movement in No. 4 being a quick one. One movement in each is in the relative major or minor. Of the 13 quick movements, three are in binary and the remainder are fugal or in ritornello form, or partake of elements of both.

Although there are four examples of normal fugal exposition, generally Handel does not attempt to write a strict fugue. Often the second entry is not an answer but another statement of the subject and the entries may appear in the violins and not in the bass. There are many instances of the opening only of the subject appearing, and the whole makes easy three-part writing with thirds and sixths the prevailing intervals. Some of the slow movements are binary, some definitely ternary, one in ritornello (first movement of No. 2) and many of the shorter movements grow out of the opening phrase and consist of a number of balanced phrases without any repetition. Such a type is the first movement of the sonata analysed below.

Sonata No. 6 in G Minor

1. *Andante*   26 bars of $\frac{4}{4}$ time

The movement opens with a striking phrase (Ex. 77) in the first violin which is repeated by the second violin, but it never reappears again.

Ex. 77

Andante

Handel, Sonata in G minor, Op. 2, No. 6
for two violins and bass
1st movement, bars 1-3

A rather hackneyed answering phrase (Ex. 78) is developed leading to a cadence at bar 12 in the relative major.

Ex.78   the same
bar 26

An arpeggio figure moves sequentially through C minor and D minor and all seems set for the return of Ex. 77, but instead a semiquaver arpeggio figure takes us through to the end. The key scheme indicates binary but the phrases develop from or contrast with preceding material. There is no double bar at the end of this movement; the second movement begins on the same bar as that in which the first movement ends.

2. *Allegro*   53 bars of $\frac{4}{4}$ time

A fugal allegro with the subject announced in the second violin. At the end of the first bar of the subject the first violin enters with a second subject. When it has finished this it has the first subject while the second violin has the second subject. The two subjects generally appear together although the first is more memorable. After the G minor exposition entries appear in D minor, F minor, D minor again, and there is a final section in the tonic.

3. *Arioso in B flat major*   55 bars of $\frac{3}{4}$ time

A ten-bar melody in the first violin repeated by the second. Bars 21–42 form a modulatory section and the main theme reappears in a shortened version followed by a coda which ends on the dominant of G minor in preparation for the next movement. Although there is little contrast of themes because the modulatory section grows out of the opening, there is a definite feeling of ternary shape.

4. *Allegro*   63 bars of $\frac{12}{8}$ time

Following the usual custom the time-signature is C although the movement is really in $\frac{12}{8}$. The movement is interesting because the repetition of each part of the binary form is written out and varied.

Bars 1–14 are the same as 14–27; 27–45 the same as 45–63. Although the harmonic background is the same, the chords are often in different positions and the triplet movement often transferred or altered. To illustrate this, the two variations of the three bars leading to the cadence of the first part of the binary movement are quoted in Ex. 79a and 79b.

Ex.79a   4th movement, bars 12–14

                                                    the same
Ex.79b   bars 25–27

Tartini 12 Trio Sonatas Op. 3

Nine of the 12 have four movements. No. 2 has three, No. 5 has two and No. 11 five. Eight begin with a slow movement and four with a quick movement. All except No. 5 have one movement (generally the slow movement) in another key. The relative is used seven times and the tonic major or minor four times. Binary is the most common form for both slow and fast movements, but there are many examples of binary expanding to ternary. The procedure is that during the second section the opening is quoted in the tonic key, sometimes the opening few bars, but often much more. There are many examples of the fugal allegro. Points of interest are:

(a) Six of the sonatas end with a dance; the minuet ending No. 9 is in rondo form.

(b) The second movement of No. 5 is in ternary form; an allegro is sandwiched between two appearances of a sarabande which itself is in binary form.

(c) No. 11 in E major has two of its movements headed Andante amoroso.

Boyce 12 Sonatas for two violins and bass

Fugue is the speciality of this set of sonatas. Boyce's fugue subjects have character and they appeal to us because of their homely English quality. Two subjects are quoted in Ex. 80.

Ex. 80a   Boyce, Sonata No. 3
Fugue subject

Ex. 80b   Boyce, Sonata No. 8
Fugue subject

Six of the movements in the odd-numbered sonatas are headed 'Fuga' and there are many other movements in fugal style. In Sonata 5 the last movement is the fugue and it is repeated in its entirety.

Four movements is the usual number but Nos. 1 and 5 each have three and No. 12 two. Ten sonatas have a movement in another key, the relative being the most common. All except Nos. 2 and 5 begin with a slow movement. The last movement is sometimes named as a dance; when it is not, it is usually light in feeling.

Ex. 81   Boyce, Sonata No. 12
Last movement (Gavotte)

Points of interest are:

No. 3 ends with minuet I – minuet II – minuet I, the first being binary and the second ternary.

No. 4 has a funeral march in E flat major, a dignified simple melody with the direction *pp* sempre.

Sonatas Nos. 6 and 11 have movements headed Affetuoso.

No. 9 has a canon 3 in 1 for its second movement.

No. 12 ends with gavotte I – gavotte II – gavotte I; both gavottes are in binary and the key of the second is the tonic minor.

The Sonatas of Bach

Any work of Bach has interest for a music student and no explanation is necessary for including all the sonatas in this brief survey. From an analysis of all of them one can arrive at Bach's procedure concerning number of movements, keys and forms. Statistics have little musical significance, but one can be sure that Bach did not work haphazardly. Maybe he did not decide on the nature of a second movement before the first was completed, and sometimes he would use material from earlier works, but the finished article would have been scrutinised and if necessary amended. The statistics given below will be of interest to those who have played or heard the works.

The works listed on page 94 total 19 sonatas. Fifteen have four movements and all keep to the pattern, slow-fast-slow-fast, except the Flute Sonata No. 1 which is fast-fast-slow-fast. The keys are varied and every one has one movement in another key, usually the relative. The only five-movement work, Violin Sonata No. 6, has two movements in another key. Of the ten sonatas in a minor key eight have a movement in the relative major, one uses the dominant minor and the other the tonic major. Nine sonatas in the major key have eight movements in the relative minor, the exception being Sonata No. 5 for unaccompanied violin which has its third movement in the subdominant major.

The forms used are varied. Many of the slow movements being short are merely the extension of the opening phrase, a very bald way of describing some of Bach's most emotional movements. They are not in binary or ternary form but there is always a balance of phrases and a ternary feeling about the use of key. A typical example is analysed at the end of the chapter.

Of the 73 movements in the works under discussion 16 (mostly slow movements) are built on an opening theme and, for want of a better word, can be called 'unary', 26 are in binary, 3 in ternary, 10 in ritornello, 14 in fugal style, 3 on a basso ostinato and one in canon. Some movements could be listed under two headings, several of the fugal movements are in Bach's fugal allegro ternary form (see *Allegro*, page 104) and ritornello and fugue are closely linked. The importance of binary is obvious, but ritornello and fugue are used more perhaps than one would have imagined.

The first of the sonatas for clavier and violin is analysed below.

Sonata No. 1 for clavier and violin in B minor

1. *Adagio*   36 bars in 6/4 time
    The keyboard begins with a 'sighing' motive (Ex. 82).

Ex.82   Bach, Sonata No. 1 for violin and clavier in B minor
Adagio   1st movement, bars 1–3

At the fifth bar the violin enters with a contrasting theme (Ex. 83).

Ex.83

the same
bars 5–7

There is a cadence in the tonic at bar 11. The violin theme is extended and it also uses that of the clavier and reaches F sharp minor at bar 20. The second part of the violin's theme, the group of short notes, is discarded, and it uses its own opening long note and the clavier's sighing motive. It takes as it were the best of both worlds and gains in importance to the end where its opening group of short notes makes a climax. The tonic key (via E minor) is reached at bar 24 and is kept to the end with a passing glance at E minor in bars 31–33.

This movement like so many of the wonderful slow movements of Bach is really a development of the opening bars with cadences occurring at almost regular intervals.

Bars 1–11 Tonic, 12–20 Dominant, 21–31 Tonic, coda 31–36. The key scheme signifies ternary form but thematically there is continual growth from the first phrase.

2. *Allegro*   141 bars of $\frac{2}{2}$ time

A fugal movement in one of Bach's usual forms. It has the ternary aspect but it is all built on the opening subjects of the first 15 bars. There are four themes, the opening subject and its bass (Ex. 84) and two counter-subjects.

Subject in bass with two counter-subjects above

After statements of these in various positions from bar 30 there is a codetta ending with a cadence in the tonic at bar 40. The opening subject with more subdued counterpoint begins in D major, but soon all the themes reappear and the music moves similarly in A major arriving at F sharp minor at bar 101 to lead the way back to B minor. The third section bar 102–141 is an exact repeat of 1–40. So there is no doubt about the ternary form but it must be stressed that there is no contrast of theme, the shape is determined by the key. To sum up:

bars 1–40 B minor main key with F sharp minor as subsidiary;
bars 41–101 D major and A major as main keys;
bars 102–141 repeat of 1–40.

3. *Andante in D major*   29 bars of $\frac{4}{4}$ time
    Like many of Bach's slow movements (of which two well-known examples are the concertos in E major and A minor for violin) this movement is built on a basso ostinato. The same bass phrase appears in various keys or begins on different notes of the scale. The ostinato is one bar of continual quaver movement and is kept with a slight occasional variation almost until the end.
    Bars 1–4 state and repeat the bass whilst the violin and upper part of the clavier have a duet. The bass is slightly altered to make a cadence.
    Bars 5–8 the opening transposed into A major.
    Bars 9–17 the same themes with cadences in B minor and F sharp minor. A link passage of two bars leads to
    Bars 19–22 a repetition of bars 1–4.
    Bars 22–29 similar to Bars 12–17 extended and changed, making the tonic the key centre and providing a climax by the bass semiquavers in bar 28 replacing the ostinato.
    This movement shows the richness of Bach's musical thought. The long flowing melody germinates from the opening bars and gradually unfolds itself with ever increasing variety. The rigidity of the bass seems not to have been a restriction but a spur to invention.

4. *Allegro*   61 bars of $\frac{3}{4}$ time
    A three-strand contrapuntal movement in binary form in which the main themes are in the first phrase. The three parts are in triple counterpoint and Bach shows the inversions. The second section of the binary movement, about twice as long as the first, has a more adventurous key-scheme. It shows the common leaning of binary towards ternary because part way through the second part there is a cadence in the tonic, and the opening bars are quoted in a modified form (due to inversion), bars 1–5 corresponding to bars 50–56.

CHAPTER TWELVE

The Early Contrapuntal Forms

Sonata form and most of the others mentioned so far in this book became established in the second part of the eighteenth and the beginning of the nineteenth centuries. The forms to be described in this chapter *Canon, Fantasia, Ricercare, Canzona,* etc., will be less familiar and they reached their peak at an earlier period. Fugue, which is an important development of these forms, has the next chapter allotted to it. These early forms are contrapuntal whereas the sonata and its allied forms are harmonic. A study of musical history is necessary to realize the difference between these styles but it is possible to describe their realizations in musical texture.

In contrapuntal style there is a combination of two or more individual lines of melody. Although each melody may have its separate existence and sound satisfactory by itself, it is the combined effect that the listener hears. The least complicated texture and the clearest to hear is two-part counterpoint. As more strands are added the weave becomes richer and more difficult to hear.

In harmonic style a melody is supported by chords. The number of notes in a chord may vary at the composer's discretion and also according to the instrument or instruments used. On a keyboard the two hands are able to play a chord of two or three notes or even one of ten or more. When a number of instruments combine, as in a string quartet, the resulting sound is described as harmonic when the interest is in the chord block, and contrapuntal when the interest is in the separate lines.

Sometimes the difference between the two is slight. It is possible to have four lines of music each with a narrow range and subdued movement, barely justifying the title of melody. The combination of these lines might appeal to one person as a succession of harmonies, and to another as four lines. But even in the most complicated counterpoint, the music stands or falls by its success or otherwise as a combination of sounds.

Although for convenience this chapter is headed 'early contrapuntal forms,' the word 'form' is not used in the same sense as it has been earlier for movements in binary or ternary form. Counterpoint is really a musical texture and the various contrapuntal 'forms' show different ways of presenting this texture. One of the obvious ways of obtaining unity in a contrapuntal texture is to give each line the same melody. So a second part would enter and repeat the opening melody; if the composition was in more than two parts other parts entered similarly. This method of composition was the stock-in-trade of music in contrapuntal style and the device of 'following my leader' is called 'imitation'. When the 'imitation' is of a special nature the composition becomes a canon or a fugue.

Canon

Canon was known originally as fuga per canonen; fuga (flight) because each voice 'flew' away from the following one which was vainly trying to catch it, and per canonen ('according to rule'), because of the rules that had to be observed in the composition. Later the words fugue and canon became separated, and described two different species of contrapuntal music.

In canon the part or parts that enter in imitation of the opening must imitate it exactly. There are several kinds of canon, the simplest being a canon 2 in 1. The first figure denotes the number of instruments or voices, or if the composition is being played on a keyboard, the number of strands of counterpoint. The second figure denotes the number of melodies imitated. In a canon 2 in 1 there are two voices and one melody, the original melody being imitated by one other voice. In canon 3 in 1 the original melody is imitated, first by one voice and then by another. A canon 4 in 2 indicates four voices and 2 different melodies, in fact two canons 2 in 1 sounding together. The second voice imitates the first at a prescribed interval and a description of a canon includes this information. A canon at the 5th above means that the second voice imitates the tune of the first a fifth higher; a canon at the 7th below, that the second voice imitates a seventh lower. When in the imitation the exact intervals are kept, the canon is said to be strict. Normally, however, canons are mostly free regarding the quality of the interval as this helps the task of modulating. Thus in a canon at the third above, if the first voice sings C E G (in the key of C) it will be answered by the second voice singing E G B. The first voice sings the interval of a major third followed by a minor third, whereas the second voice reverses the process. It is also allowable for an interval to be inflected. Thus in the key of C, C E G could be answered by E G B flat since this preserves the appearance of two successive thirds. In a canon at the unison or octave the two parts should be identical.

The distances of time at which the second voice follows the first may vary. The canon may, therefore, be at two bars' distance or at the half bar, etc. There are also different ways in which the second voice may imitate the first apart from exact imitation.

(1) Canon by inversion or canon per arsin et thesin.* The intervals are answered in the opposite direction, i.e. a rise of a fourth becomes a drop of a fourth, or a drop of a fifth becomes a rise of a fifth.

(2) Canon by augmentation. The note-lengths of the second voice are double or treble etc. those of the first. It follows that the second part lags further and further behind the first and so the canon can never be completed.

(3) Canon by diminution. The note-lengths of the second part are half or a third etc. of the first. The entry of the second voice must be considerably delayed for the device to be effective.

(4) Canon cancrizans (crab canon), canon recte et retro, and retrograde canon, all indicate a canon in which the second voice is the same as the first read backwards. In this type the two parts generally begin together.

Below are two interesting examples of the more complex type of canon by Henry Purcell.† Ex. 86 is the first four bars of

---

* This term is also used for canons in which the strong beat of the first voice is answered by a weak beat in the second voice.

† Ex. 86 and 87 are from Three Sacred Canons, Purcell (Novello). The third is a setting of an English Gloria, canon 4 in 1.

a sixteen-bar gloria of a canon 4 in 1 by inversion (per arsin et thesin).

Ex. 86 Purcell, 'Gloria Patri', Canon 4 in 1 (*per arsin et thesin*)

Ex. 87 is the first two and last two bars of a crab canon 4 in 2. The whole piece is twelve bars long but with the opening and ending put close together the canon is easier to see. The first two bars of 1st tenor are the same as the last two bars of 2nd tenor sung backwards, and the first two bars of the 2nd tenor are the same as the last two bars of the 1st tenor sung backwards. The same is true of the two bass parts. (Ex. 87)

If a canon is so constructed that when one reaches the last printed bar one can go back to the first bar and still retain the canonic effect it is described as an infinite canon or a perpetual canon.

Ex. 87 Purcell, Allelujah, Canon 4 in 2 (*recte et retro*)

The usual Latin name for the beginning voice is the *dux* or *vox antecedens* (the leader or antecedent voice) and the imitating voice is called the *comes* or *vox consequens* (the companion or consequent voice).

From the above it might be imagined that canons have little to do with music and that their chief use is in mastering contrapuntal technique. Early composers certainly fastened on to the form and made a great show of all the devices. We are too far away from the fourteenth century to be able to appreciate the caccia* or the canons of Guillaume de Machaut. The riddle canons of the fifteenth and sixteenth centuries are amusing and interesting to us, but not generally because of their musical value. In HAM I 66 is an example from Dufay's Mass, *L'homme armé*, the Agnus

* A strict canon 2 in 1 at about eight bars distance to texts describing hunting scenes. An example is recorded in Oxford History of Music in Sound.

Dei is in canon and a Latin inscription in riddle form is above the music which, when solved, would give the type of canon. Palestrina's★ 'Missa ad Fugam in perpetuo Canone' shows to what heights canonic writing can rise. This is a complete setting of the Mass in three, four, and five parts, every movement in some form of canon. The technique is masterly and the work is admired not because it is in canon but because it is great music. The same applies to the Goldberg variations of Bach where nine canons can be found at every interval from the unison to the ninth including two (at the fourth and fifth) in contrary motion.

Canon in short spells is often used during the course of a symphonic or sonata movement. The melodies closely following each other create a tension and give fresh musical interest to the homophonic form. It seems to take its place quite naturally even when it comes in the middle of a symphony. Sometimes the canon is so short that it hardly justifies the use of the word, so the phrase 'canonic imitation' is used instead. An example is taken from Brahms's *Requiem* at the beginning of the recapitulation of the fifth movement (bar 62). The canonic imitation is in augmentation at the octave between the solo soprano and chorus tenors.

Ex. 88

Andante
Soprano Solo

Brahms, Requiem
Movement 5, bars 63 and 64

Chorus Tenor

Orchestral Bass

Well known instances of canon are Bach, Et in unum dominum, (B minor Mass), Art of Fugue, Canonic variations for organ on Vom Himmel hoch and other chorale preludes, Musical Offering; Mozart, 'Prague' Symphony, second movement; Beethoven, Symphony No. 4, first movement, 32 variations in C minor; Schumann Op. 56 studies for pedal piano; César Franck Symphony first and last movements, Sonata for violin and piano, last movement.

★ Quoted in full in *Der Kanon*, ein Singbuch für Alle. F. Jöde Moseler Verlag Wolfenbüttel.

Round

A round is a vocal canon at the unison for a stated number of voices. When the first voice reaches the end it goes back to the beginning, likewise with the remaining voices except the last which need go through the piece once only. To make a successful ending the number of repeats must be agreed by the singers. A round is not normally written out in full but the voices are placed one below the other, so a round for three voices looks like a three-part composition. Most rounds are unaccompanied, but mention must be made of the accompanied one in Beethoven's *Fidelio* 'Mir ist so wunderbar'. A round might seem out of place in an opera, especially as in this case the four characters sing different words to the same music; however its effect is most dramatic.

Catch

A catch is a species of round common in England in the seventeenth and eighteenth centuries. The voices followed each other as in a round, but the words were so contrived to make a comical effect or a double entendre. For instance, 'How Sophia' becomes 'house a-fire'; but this is a mild good-mannered example; in many the words have had to be replaced for modern publication.

Other contrapuntal forms which preceded fugue were fancy (or fantasia), ricercar, canzona and capriccio. Composers used these words but it is difficult to find the difference between them. Their common link is that they were written at the time when instrumental music was beginning to lose its dependence on vocal music. In the motets of the fourteenth and fifteenth centuries there are sections without words and it is generally presumed that these sections were played by instruments. We know that the English madrigals were played on viols* and Whythorne's Duos (1590) have as a sub-title 'playne and easie to be sung or played on musicall instruments'. On the continent instrumental canzonas were being written, imitating the short settings of poems by the Netherland masters. The French chanson

* 'The first appearance of "apt for viols and voices" is in Weelkes third book of Madrigals, 1600'. (*The English Fantasy Suite*, Cecily Arnold and Marshall Johnson. Proceedings of the Royal Musical Association 1955–56.)

(canzona francese) with its clear form was much copied in Italy and the publications are even named Canzoni alla Francese or Canzoni da sonare in distinction to the works which were sung. So the instrumental style grew up with, and out of, the vocal.

The opening musical phrase in vocal music was generally short and so the first group of imitative entries lasted only for a few bars. Before the last voice had finished its first entry the voice that began would already be on its second phrase. These compositions were made up of a series of interlocked sections called 'points', each point depending for its shape and length on the words. When instruments replaced voices the same method of composing was used, but as instrumental style developed so the phrases were made longer. The length of the musical phrase was not now governed by the verbal phrase and composers were able to lengthen it.

Canzona

The canzona which was written for clavier or for groups of instruments had a number of short sections, each elaborating a theme. The themes were not always different, sometimes they were related to each other as in Ex. 89, or sometimes the sections were repeated as in HAM 78, an instrumental canzona by Obrecht. The themes were generally in quicker notes and the style less severe than the ricercar (see page 115). The development of the instrumental and keyboard species is beyond the scope of this book but in brief it can be said that during the first half of the seventeenth century the instrumental type showed itself as the forerunner of the sonata da chiesa and the keyboard type the forerunner of the fugue. Frescobaldi (1593–1643) excelled in both types and one of his keyboard works is analysed. (Ex. 89 a-e).

There are five sections; the first in $\frac{4}{4}$ time (14 bars), the second $\frac{6}{4}$ (9 bars and 2 bars of $\frac{4}{4}$), the third $\frac{4}{4}$ (19 bars), the fourth a mixture of $\frac{6}{4}$ and $\frac{3}{4}$ (17 bars also with 4 bars of $\frac{4}{4}$), the fifth in $\frac{4}{4}$ (24 bars). The effect of the $\frac{4}{4}$ bars at the end of the second and fourth sections is to broaden the cadence (a common device with Frescobaldi) and lead into the new section. The beginnings of each of the sections are quoted and each continues with further entries

Frescobaldi, Canzona from the Second book of Toccatas

Ex.89a
bars 1–4

Ex.89b
the same
2nd section, bar 15

Ex.89c
the same
3rd section, bar 26

Ex.89d
the same
4th section, bar 45

Ex.89e
the same
5th section, bar 65

of the opening theme. Each successive section is a variant on the first and is an early example of what was later known as 'cyclic form'.* The last section closely resembles the first but is more intense because much is made of the inversion of the counter-theme that accompanies the main one.

* See Chapter Eleven, Exs. 73–76, also Chapter Seven.

Fantasia

The title Fantasia when applied to the lute or keyboard instruments of the sixteenth and seventeenth centuries covered a variety of forms and included the arrangement of vocal pieces for the lute and programme music such as the Fantasia by William Mundy (*Fitzwilliam Virginal Book*). This has as its sub-headings Faire Wether, Lightning, Thunder, Calme Wether. When applied to instrumental ensemble there seems little to distinguish it from the ricercar; since the chief composers were English, they preferred the word fancy. The earliest is a 'fansie' of Mr. Newman's in the *Mulliner Book*.* Morley in his *Plaine and Easie Introduction to Practical Musicke* (1597) says that in the fantasie 'may more art be showne than in any other musicke' and describes it by saying that 'a musician taketh a point at his pleasure, and wresteth and turneth it as he list, making either much or little of it according as shall seeme best in his own conceit'. Like the canzona it had a number of sections each built on a theme developed contrapuntally. Fancies were composed during the seventeenth century, the last and greatest being those by Purcell written in the 1670s.†

Ricercar

The Flemish composer Willaert uses the two words ricercar and fantasia for his 'Fantasie Ricercari contrapunti a 3 voci' (1559). These works are imitative of the sixteenth century motet. The earliest use of the word ricercar is in Petrucci's lute books 1507–8. It describes pieces that could be named as studies, works demanding a high standard of technique. The real meaning of the word, 'recherché' or something 'sought out', was shown in the works written later in the century. In the ricercars we find (as in the fantasies) examples of augmentation, diminution, inversion and other contrapuntal ingenuities. During the seventeenth century the ricercar often used one theme rather than a number of 'points', thus showing itself as a forerunner of the fugue.

* A collection of varied pieces by many composers compiled by Mulliner during the third quarter of the sixteenth century.
† The history of the fancie is dealt with in *English Chamber Music*, Meyer, London 1946.

An example of a ricercar by Johann Krieger (1649–1725) is given in HAM 249. It is built on one theme and opens like a normal fugue.* After all the voices have entered the three upper voices re-enter with inversions of the theme and the remainder has entries either direct or inverted.

A ricercar by Frescobaldi in the *First Book of Capriccios*, 1626, is similar to a fugue with episodes. It is 86 bars long and the interest is maintained by the introduction of counter-subjects. The subject is given in Ex. 90. There are 28 entries either as written or beginning on the note B. The subject is of limited range descending twice to its opening note, so the episodes with wider sweep and movement bring welcome relief.

Ex.90 Ricercar from First Book of Capriccios (*1626*)
bars 1–3

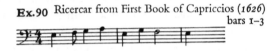

Bach uses the word ricercar in the *Musical Offering* to describe two fugues, Fuga (Ricercata) a 3 voci and Fuga (Ricercata) a 6 voci. He makes an acrostic of the word in the title 'Regis Iussu Cantio Et Reliqua Canonica Arte Resoluta' (the theme given by the command of the king and the remainder resolved according to canonic style). In Bach's time it seems that the word was used for music in a strict contrapuntal style.

Capriccio

The capriccio has no special characteristic to distinguish it from the early forms already described. Frescobaldi sometimes gives a title that suggests that the freedom inherent in the name might be more in the invention of the theme than in its working out. (Capriccio pastorale, Capriccio sopra il cucu.) The word is mainly remembered today for Bach's 'Capriccio on the absence of his well-beloved brother', a piece of programme music written in 1704 in six movements each with a title.

---

* See Chapter Thirteen.

Toccata

Although the toccata can hardly be considered as an early contrapuntal form it has been mentioned in this chapter in connection with Ex. 89 and it is convenient to explain it here. The word means 'touched' and is used in the same sense as the French word 'touché'. The keys were touched (toccata), the strings were sounded (sonata), and the voices sang (cantata). The early toccatas had alternating sections of quick passages and imitative sections (see HAM 153, *Toccata* by Merulo, 1533–1604). The form was developed by the North German organists, Buxtehude, Bruhns and Bach, into a fine rhapsodic movement and the sectional treatment of Merulo was often retained. Bach used it as a movement preceding a fugue and treats it freely, sometimes sectionally and sometimes as a huge structure, as in the Toccata in F which is analysed below.

A¹ Bars	1–55	A canon at the octave at 2 bars' distance between the right hand and the left hand over a tonic pedal. A third part added at bar 35.
	55–82	Pedal solo built on canonic theme with a 2-bar cadential figure on the manuals.
A²	83–176 (dominant)	Similar to 1–82 but now in the dominant. The hands reverse in the canon and the 2-bar cadential figure is extended to 8 bars in the pedal and imitated by the hands.
B¹	176–218 (modulatory)	A 4-bar mounting arpeggio phrase. It is built out of a figure from the pedal solo (bars 64–65). There are five appearances with an 8-bar interrupted cadence (bars 197–204) and the figure is further developed.
A³	218–238 D minor	Three-part invertible counterpoint on opening figure.
B²	238–270 (modulatory)	Six-fold appearance of mounting figure with an 8-bar cadence.
A⁴	270–290 A minor	Same as 218–238 except that the parts are inverted, the middle part becoming the bass.

B3	290–332 (modulatory)	Five-fold appearance of mounting figure with 8-bar cadence interrupted and extended.
A5	332–352	Same as 218–238 except that parts are inverted, the treble becoming the bass.
B4	353–438 modulatory (ending sub- dominant, dominant and tonic)	The mounting figure is extended and reaches a dominant pedal for 30 bars (bars 394–433) culminating in the 8-bar cadential figure. This is interrupted to reach the tonic via G flat major, A flat major, B flat minor and a Neapolitan sixth cadence.

At its first two appearances B¹ and B² are 32 bars long. B3 extends to 42 and B4, making the climax, to 86. The student should analyse the extended cadential phrases and observe the use of interrupted cadences. The work grows out of the opening bar; the whole is there in embryo except for the cadential phrases.

Chapter Thirteen

Fugue

Fugue reached its highest point in the works of Bach. He was able to make it express all shades of feeling. Whilst this was achieved to a certain extent by some of his predecessors, it is Bach who towers above them all. He gathers to himself the accumulated contrapuntal experience of many centuries and his fertile brain is able to mould it to one end—musical expressiveness. His technique is so masterly that the most difficult contrapuntal feats may pass unnoticed because the listener is mesmerised by some great emotional outburst.

Every fugue of Bach is different because first, the emotional course is determined by his view of the character of the subject and second, the contrapuntal treatment is varied according to the subject's contrapuntal propensity.

Fugue is not really a form, it is an ordered way of presenting a contrapuntal texture. This texture may be finely or loosely woven and the pattern made by the strands may be described. But this describes a method of writing, 'the fugal method', and not a form. The keys used may suggest ways in which a fugue may be divided and it is possible in this way to describe some of the '48' as binary or ternary in form. Each fugue is a separate entity making a unique growth from its subject. The fugue analysed at the end of the chapter has been chosen for the purpose of showing as much of the fugal method as possible, but as mentioned above the analysis will apply only to this particular fugue. The only satisfactory way of realising the extent of Bach's genius is to analyse the whole of the '48'.*

A fugue is written for a definite number of voices and although during the course of a fugue one or more voices may rest it is not possible to add voices. The word 'voice' describes each

* If necessary with the help of Professor Tovey in the Associated Board edition.

strand of the fugue. Originally fugues were vocal, but the word
'voice' is used even when fugues are instrumental.

The Exposition

The exposition is that section at the beginning of a fugue in
which all the voices sing the main theme (the subject). Every
fugue opens with an exposition, but after that there is no fixed
plan. The fugal exposition is like the imitative opening of the
sixteenth century motet in which the theme is altered to suit the
pitch of the voices. In a four-voice fugue using soprano, alto,
tenor and bass it was necessary to have only two different starting
notes. The range of a soprano was about the same as a tenor
although an octave higher, and an alto the same as a bass (an
octave higher). This will be seen in Ex. 91.

Ex. 91   Tye, 'Praise the Lord ye Children'
                                                bars 1–6

Although Ex. 91 is not a fugue the opening would satisfy the requirements of a fugal exposition, as in fact would openings of most fancies, ricercars and canzonas (compare Ex. 89). The opening phrase is named the subject and the transposed version the answer; the third entry is that of the subject and the fourth the answer. The answer then is the subject transposed up a fifth or down a fourth. This gives a general picture of the exposition but its parts are now considered in more detail.

The Subject

A good subject is easily remembered because of some characteristic feature of melody or rhythm or both. The expressive quality or musical character of the subject foreshadows the emotional course of the fugue and the subject must be appropriately designed for any contrapuntal device the composer wishes to use. Bach uses stretto only when it goes naturally, which is another way of saying that he designed the subject to go in stretto. The subject will establish the tonic key but it sometimes modulates to the dominant. *Exs. 92–95 show different types of subjects.

Bach, 48 Preludes and Fugues, I. 7
bars 1–4

Ex. 92 Subject

Answer

* These examples are from the '48' and the normal way of numbering the Preludes and Fugues is to use I for the first book and II for the second book followed by the number of the Fugue in arabic.

The Answer

The second voice enters with the answer which may or may not be an exact transposition of the subject. If it is exact, the answer is 'real'; if it is altered at its opening, the answer is 'tonal'.

To understand the reasons for a tonal answer it is necessary to look at the origin of fugue.

As was mentioned earlier, the fugal exposition derived from the imitative opening of the motet at a period before the major and minor scales were evolved. Compositions were written not in a key but in a mode. In a mode the two most important notes were the final (the note we would name as tonic) and the dominant, generally, but not always, the fifth note of the mode. In order to preserve the mode the two important notes had to be prominent, so when the first voice began on the final the imitating voice would begin on the dominant. When the first voice began on the dominant the imitation would begin on the final. In the early days then, the answer was still in the mode and was merely the subject at a different pitch.*

The early imitative procedure was still kept when the modes were replaced by diatonic scales. So in fugue, if the subject begins on the dominant, the answer will begin on the tonic.

Exs. 92 and 93 are instances of a subject beginning on a dominant.

A tonal answer is also necessary when the subject (i) leaps from tonic to dominant at its opening (Ex. 94a) or (ii) the dominant note is brought into prominence at the beginning of the subject (Ex. 94b). In these cases the dominant is answered by the tonic.

The inheritance of the modes is probably responsible for the fact that so few of Bach's subjects modulate; there are hardly any that do so in the '48'. When the subject modulates to the dominant another adjustment of the notes is necessary. This change is called a 'mutation'. The same subject can involve two adjustments as in Ex. 92, where at the opening the dominant is answered by the tonic and the point of mutation occurs after the rest. The interval of a second in the subject, b' flat to a' natural (tenth to eleventh note), has been altered to a third, f' to d', in the answer.

* The above over-simplifies the problem and what took many years to evolve cannot be described in a few words. The interested reader is advised to study the chapter on the 'Answer' in *The Technique and Spirit of Fugue* by George Oldroyd (Oxford University Press). The answer is considered historically and the whole question of tonal and real answers thoroughly discussed.

The reason for the necessity of mutation in a subject modulating to the dominant is obvious. If, as in Ex. 92, the answer beginning in B flat were to modulate to F, the next entry of the subject in key E flat would be difficult to make sound convincing.

It must be stressed that although the answer is a fifth higher than the subject it is not necessarily in the key of the dominant. Very often it was Bach's practice to leave the main cadence in the dominant until the end of the exposition. The answer would be in the key of the tonic with a passing reference to the dominant soon neutralised by the return of the subject. In Ex. 92, the answer is in the tonic and there is no doubt that the whole of the exposition centres round the tonic key. In Exs. 94 and 95 the answer begins in the tonic, Ex. 94(b) remaining in it for most of the time. In Fugue II, 9, (Ex. 95,) the nearest the exposition gets to the key of the dominant (apart from its final cadence) is in bar 3.

There are other variants in the answer that are occasionally met with. The answer may be a fourth higher instead of a fifth and is therefore known as a subdominant answer.* The entries may not be in the usual order. In I, 1, the order is subject, answer, answer, subject.

The answer may come in one of three places: (1) immediately at the end of the subject; (2) before the subject is finished; or (3) some time after it has finished. If it comes at (3) then obviously there must be a linking phrase to join the end of the subject to the answer. This phrase is named 'codetta' by some writers and 'episode' by others. (During the remainder of the fugue the freer sections between appearances of the subject are named episodes and the only reason against using that name for a similar section in the exposition is that it is generally shorter.) The codetta or episode† is more commonly found between the second and third entries (i.e. between the answer and the subject) than at the end of the subject. Its purpose is to provide some relief

---

* Discussed at length in *The Spirit and Technique of Fugue.*

† R. O. Morris *The Structure of Music*, Oxford 1935, suggests that codetta might be used of a short link that is purely tonal in function and episode for a longer and more definitely constructive section. Tovey in his article on fugue in *Encyclopaedia Britannica* does not use the word codetta but only episode.

after two appearances of the theme. Ex. 92 (I, 7) shows under the bracketed section 'a', a link between the subject and answer and Ex. 93 (I, 16) a link between the answer and subject. Many of the '48' show much longer sections, for example II, 11 in F major, bars 9–14. The codetta usually grows out of the subject, as in Ex. 93 (I, 16) and II, 11.

The Countersubject (abbreviated below to CS)

As the second voice sings the answer, the first voice can sing either a free part against it or a CS. One cannot tell which it is until one has heard (or looked at) the next entry of the subject. If the melody then sung by the second voice is a transposed version of that sung by the first voice earlier, then that melody is a CS. It will also occur in later parts of the fugue. If it appears with every entry of subject and answer it is termed a regular CS. Since it will have to appear either below or above the subject, it is so constructed that the subject makes a satisfactory bass to it and vice versa. This kind of two-part writing is known as 'double counterpoint'. The CS should have an individual character that makes it easily recognisable. It should also be contrasted to the subject and yet be in the same style and preserve the overall mood of the fugue.

Sometimes there are two CSs. In this case the second CS is sung by the first voice, while the second voice has the first CS and the third voice the subject. This would normally be in triple counterpoint, i.e. each of the three lines would be satisfactory as a bass part.

With two CSs the later presentations of the subject can be well varied. There are three possible bass lines, each with two different arrangements of the upper parts making six different positions in all.

Two examples of CS from the '48' are:

(a) I, 7 (Ex. 92, bracketed CS). The CS has quavers against the subject's semiquavers and vice versa, a common way of obtaining contrast.

(b) I, 16 (Ex. 93 bracketed CS). The CS is a modified inversion of the subject in reverse.

Fugues having two CSs are I, 2, 3, 21; II, 17. There is an example of three CSs in I, 12, but Bach for obvious musical reasons does not show the 24 available positions.

Redundant Entry

When all the voices have entered there is sometimes an extra entry of the subject or answer known as a redundant entry. It enables the CS to be heard in a different position. If the fugue has begun with the soprano voice and each entry has been lower, the CS will always be above the subject; so in the redundant entry the CS can be shown below. Similarly if the order of entries is upwards from the bass, the CS will always be below the subject and the redundant entry gives an opportunity for the CS to be above.

I, 7 begins with the subject in the soprano and a redundant entry in the soprano at bars 11 and 12 enables the CS to be heard below it.

II, 23 begins with the subject in the bass and there is a redundant entry at bar 19 to enable the CS to be heard above it.

Counter-exposition

Sometimes there are two or three redundant entries, II, 17 for instance has three. When every voice sings the subject and answer again so that there is a complete second exposition, it is known as a counter-exposition. It is not a repeat of the first because often the voice that had the subject, now has the answer (but see the examples below). It is unusual for the first voice to sing the subject in the counter-exposition unaccompanied. A counter-exposition often occurs when the subject is short, but this is not necessarily a deciding factor. The two expositions strongly emphasise the tonic key. Examples of counter-exposition are:

(a) I, 1. The entries in the first exposition are subject (alto), answer (soprano), answer (tenor), subject (bass); in the counter-exposition the order is subject (soprano), answer (tenor), answer (alto), answer (bass).

(b) I, 9. In the first exposition the order is subject (alto), answer (soprano), subject (bass); in the counter-exposition subject (soprano), answer (alto), answer (bass).

Other devices used in a counter-exposition are stretto (for definition see pp. 127 & 128); II, 9, and inversion I, 15. In I, 15 not only is the subject inverted but also its accompanying CS.

The remainder of the Fugue

After the exposition has ended there is no invariable procedure. The exposition is bound by rules to a certain extent. Every voice must sing the subject or answer, but the order of entry is not fixed and there may or may not be a CS. But when each voice has entered, every fugue becomes a special case. There will be further entries of the subject and answer and they will often be in keys other than tonic and dominant to obtain variety. For the same reason there may be sections where the subject does not appear. Somewhere towards the end the tonic key has to gain precedence to make a satisfactory conclusion. To give a sense of musical growth, the musical material has to evolve from the germinal subject and there should be a series of climactic points. All this has to be achieved through counterpoint. The above would fit as a rough description of any fugue and he would be a bold person who, with Bach's fugues in mind, would attempt to go much further. There are, however, certain technical words to be defined. The reader must be warned that all that is described below occurs in no one fugue but that some of it occurs in some fugues!

Middle Entries are those occurring after the exposition and before the final entry or entries with the tonic as centre. They may occur singly or as subject and answer, or as two or more subjects. They are sometimes in related keys and sometimes in tonic and dominant. Tonic and dominant are not always left behind once the exposition is over. These keys are used, for instance, in the first four fugues of book I. Middle entries may occur in augmentation (II, 2, bar 19), diminution (II, 9, bar 26), or inversion (I, 15, bar (20). These three devices were explained in relation to canon (p. 108). The subject may also appear in stretto.

Stretto is the subject in canonic imitation. It rarely lasts for more than a few bars. One voice begins the subject and before it is finished a second voice interrupts with another statement of it.

The imitation may be between two or more voices. The last

voice would normally have the subject in full. The earlier voice(s) might have only part and each is free to go its own way as soon as the next voice has taken over. A long overlap gives a greater feeling of stretto than a short one. There are exceptional cases where every voice has the whole of a subject and the stretto is complete. It warrants its description as a 'stretto maestrale' (a masterly stretto). Ex. 96 shows one from II, 5 (bars 45–46). It is a close stretto and each appearance of the subject is on a different note.

Ex.96

II. 5
bars 45–46

All subjects will not go easily in stretto and it seems to be Bach's method either to use stretto a great deal or to avoid it. When he wrote a subject he presumably knew its capabilities. Having decided on stretto as a feature of the fugue he used it throughout, sometimes even in the exposition (see II, 9).*

Episode

Technically, any section of the fugue in which the subject does not appear is an episode, although as mentioned on p. 124, the word codetta is often used for such places in the exposition and the word coda is used for what appears after the last entry. Episodes provide contrasting sections to the subject and they may be modulatory, leading into a new key for the next entry. The musical material may be a development of some phrase already

---

* Many students seem to imagine that stretto occurs in all fugues and is always used at the end of a fugue. This is quite at variance with the practice of Bach.

heard or it may be new. Bach often uses modulatory sequences and writes in double counterpoint. This enables the same episode to be used later inverted.

Final Section

The description is given to that part at the end of the fugue where the subject reappears in the tonic key. There may be one or more entries of subject and answer and quite often the entries are in stretto. After the final entry there may be a coda.★

Every fugue has an exposition followed by middle entries and the final section. On the face of it it looks therefore as if fugue could be ternary in form. However, when one examines the '48' there are very few that could be so described. Each makes a unique growth after the exposition. Bach also frequently uses tonic and dominant in the middle entries, which is not usual practice in a ternary shape, and few fugues have a well-defined final section. Bach was quite capable of writing in ternary form and the reader will remember that the fugal allegro of the sonata was generally in a definite ternary shape. One can only say that he did not do so usually in his fugues. The most that can be said is that the fugue will end in the key it began in and usually finishes with an entry of the subject.

Two fugues amongst others which show a definite ternary shape are I, 16, and II, 18, and two that show binary are I, 6, and II, 21. Most are without definite breaks as I, 11 and II, 12. In I, 11, a fugue concerned mainly with stretto at the octave at 2 bars distance, there is a cadence after a group of entries in D minor (bar 46), another after a group in G minor, an episode of 9 bars leading to an ornamented extended form of the subject in the tonic and the fugue ends.

Other species of fugal writing are:

Double Fugue

A fugue on two subjects. They may be announced together or there may be two distinct expositions.

★ Sometimes the last entry comes in the coda as in the Great G major organ fugue, the last entry being in the subdominant.

The first is not favoured by Bach and there are no examples in the fugues of the '48' but one of the preludes I, 7, has a section in this form. The organ works have some examples, the most well known being the fugue in C minor following the Passacaglia. Apart from Bach, there is the Kyrie from Mozart's *Requiem Mass*, No. 52 of Handel's *Judas Maccabeus* (the second part of the chorus, We worship God), and No. 32 of Beethoven's *Diabelli* variations. The second type with two distinct expositions is shown in II, 4 and 18. In both of these the second exposition follows after the first has been developed.

Triple Fugue

A fugue on three subjects. Bach announces the subjects separately as in I, 4 and II, 14. In I, 4 the three subjects appear at bars 1, 35 and 49; in II, 14, at bar 1–20 and 36.

The well-known St. Anne Fugue for organ is in three sections with three subjects but, although the first and second and the first and third combine, the three never come together.

Fugue on a Chorale

A composition for organ or voices in which each line of a chorale-melody is treated fugally. There are many examples in the Bach organ works and church cantatas. The opening voice has a theme derived from the first line of the chorale, often in some form of diminution, and the remaining voices enter fugally except the last which has the melody from which the fugue subject was derived. Sometimes the melody is in long notes like a sixteenth-century canto fermo. The second line of the chorale is similarly treated and so on to the end. A well-known example is the chorale prelude 'Wenn wir in höchsten nöthen sein'.* Another example is the first movement of the cantata 'Ein' feste Burg'. Each of the four voices takes part in the fugal expositions. At the close of each exposition the chorale melody appears in canon in the orchestra. Bach in his generous way also writes an independent orchestral accompaniment.

---

* The chorale-prelude also known as *Vor deinen Thron* BWV 668 and usually played on the organ at the conclusion of an instrumental performance of the Art of Fugue.

Fughetta

A short fugue. The exposition being over, there is not much to follow. There are many in the Bach organ works and while some are extremely short others are longer. One of the best is the fughetta on the choral 'Dies sind die heil'gen zehn Gebot' for manuals alone. It is in $\frac{12}{8}$ time and lasts 35 bars. There is a normal exposition in four parts and after one bar extension of the answer there are four middle entries inverted in stretto. The last phrase of the inversion is taken as material for a long episode of 13 bars and the subject comes in stretto between the outside parts. The work ends with the last note of the subject. (Ex. 97 quotes the last 2½ bars.) In the works of Bach there is not always a distinction between 'fuga' and 'fughetta'. Some of the movements labelled 'fuga' are shorter than those labelled 'fughetta'.

Ex. 97   Bach, Fughetta on 'Dies sind die Heil'gen zehn gebot'
bars 33–35

Fugato (literally 'fugued')

A short section of a piece that begins like a fugal exposition but does not maintain it. It occurs in non-fugal works such as sonata, symphony, chamber music or opera. It may be short as in the last movement of Beethoven's Sonata Op. 10, No. 2, or long as in the last movement of the string quartet Op. 59, No. 3.

Accompanied Fugue

A fugue for voices with independent accompaniment for orchestra. The accompaniment has independent sections but it often doubles some of the voice parts. In Brahms's *Requiem* the two choruses 'But the righteous souls' and 'Worthy art Thou' are so constructed. The fugal writing for the voices is not affected but the orchestra is able to emphasise the climactic points. The fugues in later oratorios are generally more free, as the demons chorus from Elgar's *Gerontius* (Dispossessed, aside thrust) and the Sanctus in Verdi's *Requiem*.

Fugue after Bach

With the rise of the sonata attention was given to the contrast of themes rather than in the development of one. Fugal texture was no longer necessary; it was often a hindrance in the new style but composers still used it for special purposes. Church music, always conservative, was composed in contrapuntal style. Fugues are found in the masses of Haydn, Mozart and Beethoven. On the few occasions when Mozart indulged in fugal writing he showed that he had a technique second to none.* The music of the Three Armed Men in *The Magic Flute*, which is as near a fugue on a chorale as one can get, always surprises by its likeness to Bach. Beethoven in his third period found the contrapuntal idiom suited to his utterances and fugue reappears in fresh surroundings. Using all the contrapuntal devices of the earlier period, he imbued the fugue with a depth and mystery never found before or since. He bent the form to his emotional needs. He gave himself many handicaps through using inversion, augmentation and diminution, as if he had to battle with intractable material to bring out his greatest powers. The fugue at the end of the Piano Sonata Op. 106 (*Hammerclavier*) reaches out to the limits with its subject in cancrizans and is difficult to play and understand. The two fugues in Op. 110 are easier for the ordinary mortal to appreciate and to play. What a seemingly impossible plan for a movement is the last of Op. 110. An introduction in recitative style in A flat major leading to an arioso dolente in A flat minor, a fugue in A flat major, the arioso repeated in G minor and the fugue again, this time inverted in G major, leading to a big climax in A flat major with the subject the right way round. All the contrapuntal devices are there. The subject appears plain or augmented or diminished or combined with itself in inversion and the tension never relaxes.

---

* One can imagine his excitement when he heard Bach's *Singet dem Herrn* in the Thomaskirche at Leipzig in 1789, for the first time.

Other fugues of Beethoven are to be found in the C sharp minor quartet Op. 131, the Mass in D and the Grosse Fuge Op. 133.

Since Beethoven, many composers have written fugues in choral works and organ pieces: Mendelssohn, 'Elijah', 42nd Psalm, 6 Preludes and Fugues; Schumann, 6 Fugues on B A C H ; Liszt, Prelude and Fugue B A C H; Brahms, Fugue in A flat minor, *Requiem*; Verdi, *Requiem* and *Falstaff*. Examples for piano are more rare: Mendelssohn, 6 Preludes and Fugues for Piano Op. 35; Brahms, Variations on a Theme of Handel; Franck, Prelude Choral and Fugue. Fugues that have been written for orchestra: Weinberger, Fugue from *Schwanda the Bagpipe*; Britten, Fugue from the *Young Person's Guide to the Orchestra*; Walton, Spitfire Prelude and Fugue; Bloch, Concerto Grosso No. 1. Twelve note music makes much use of contrapuntal texture. Having once established the row it becomes the basis of the composition and is repeated on different notes and varied by the old contrapuntal devices of augmentation, diminution, and inversion.

Composers in all ages have been drawn to contrapuntal writing and there is every evidence that this will continue.

Below a complete fugue, I, 2 is analysed. It is hoped that the reader will analyse the remainder of the '48'.

Fugue I, 2, in C minor
Bars:

1–3 Subject in alto ending on first note of third bar.

3–5 Answer in soprano (tonal because the fourth note is altered), alto has first CS.

5–6 Codetta built on opening phrase of subject in soprano and alto basing its figure on the last phrase of subject. This is written in double counterpoint at the 12th.*

7–9 Subject in bass, CS1 treble, CS2 in alto.

9–11 Sequential episode modulating to E flat via B flat. The top two voices answer each other sequentially. The bass derives its running semiquavers from CS1.

11–13 First middle entry in relative major in soprano, alto has CS2, bass CS1.

* See Glossary.

13-15 An episode which modulates to C minor, the soprano inverting bars 9-10, the alto and bass being derived from CS1 and CS2 respectively.

15-17 Second middle entry in G minor (but it begins in C minor) in alto with soprano having CS1 and bass CS2.

17-18 Episode. The same material is used in 17-18 as 5-6. The soprano of 5-6 is now in the bass and the alto shows the inversion at the 12th. The soprano moves in thirds with the bass.

18-20 Shows an inversion of 17-18, the alto and bass changing over.

20-22 Third middle entry in C minor, an inversion of bars 7-9.

22-26 Episode as 9-11 developed and extended and emphasising the dominant to prepare the way for

26-29 Final entry in bass with CS1 in alto and CS2 in treble. An additional half bar makes a perfect cadence in tonic.

29-31 Entry in soprano over a pedal bass giving the effect of a coda. The contrapuntal writing gives way to harmonic, and chords punctuate the subject.

This fugue has no stretti and the middle entries are in the relative major, the dominant and the tonic. The two CSs with the consequent triple counterpoint, the derivation of the episodes from the CSs and the relationship of the episodes to each other give unity to the fugue.

CHAPTER FOURTEEN

Air With Variations

Air with Variations is not strictly a form, it is a number of
different presentations of a theme. The air or theme is generally
in binary or ternary form and is normally short, and some of the
variations usually keep the structure of the theme.

Variation has a long history and the repetition of a tune
with some differences was one of the obvious ways of composition. Even in a folk song the fact that each verse had different
words, often portraying a different mood, must have caused the
singer to improvise a varied melodic line. The mediaeval use of
a tune, sacred or secular, as the basis of the settings of the mass,
made these works appear as a species of variation. The tune,
known as the 'cantus firmus', was often put in an inside part and
lost what rhythm it had by appearing in long notes. The words
enabled it to be recognised.

Examples of variations in the first part of the sixteenth century
are given in HAM Nos. 103 and 122. No. 103 is for virginals
and is built on a four-bar 'basso ostinato'. The literal translation
'obstinate bass' is self-explanatory. In this piece the bass appears
twelve times with a varied right hand. The use of a constant bass
part with varied upper parts was a normal method of composition
for another 200 years. HAM 122 is a set of variations for lute
by Luis de Narvaez. There are five variations on a theme about
16 bars long. Each variation is a separate section with a description.
The main differences are in the position of the melody, which is
in the bass as well as the treble, and in the tempo.

These examples show the two main early species of variations.
The first with its repetitive bass and the second where each
variation is a self-contained section. It is the second, where the
theme is normally recognisable in an upper part, that is generally

regarded as the real 'Air with Variations' which came to its full flowering in classical times. The first, which includes ground bass and passacaglia, is no less an example of the variation principle because it was used mainly before the classical era. Before describing these species separately an example of an Elizabethan set of variations will be analysed.

The English virginal composers wrote many sets of variations on sacred or secular tunes. In addition, one of the common methods of composing was to repeat and embellish each section of a piece. For instance, *The Duke of Brunswick's Alman* by John Bull★ is in five sections and can be represented as A¹ A² B¹ B² B³. The repetition of A and the two repetitions of B are in quicker notes, but in all the variations the harmony is unchanged. The basic harmony was retained even in the very long sets of variations. The opening piece of the *Fitzwilliam Virginal Book* is a set of variations on *Walsingham* by John Bull, one of the foremost virtuosi of the day. He tried out new patterns of keyboard technique, some of which are very awkward, and others fore-shadow nineteenth-century piano writing. Walsingham was well enough known in its day for Shakespeare to introduce it into *Hamlet*.

Ex. 98   Walsingham, An old English Melody

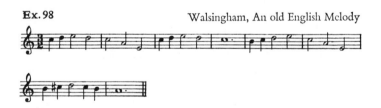

Notice the similarity between each half, bars 2 and 5 being the same. In each variation the melody or an ornamented version of it is always in the treble and the harmony is basically the same. There are 29 variations, so the piece with its lack of harmonic variety makes heavy going today.† To show Bull's

★ From the Fitzwilliam Virginal Book.
† In performance it is wise to choose a few variations rather than perform the entire set, unless one is playing to a special audience. Possibly this was done in Bull's day, as a selection of the variations appears in a MS in Christ Church Library, Oxford.

methods and his brilliance as a technician, the opening of a
selected number of variations is printed below. One must bear
in mind that at this period keyboard technique had not been
established and that Bull was a pioneer. (Ex. 99)

Another species of variations was the Ground Bass. As its
name implies it is a bass phrase which is repeated and the upper
parts vary. It was known also as Ground or later as Basso ostinato.

John Bull, Walsingham from
Fitzwilliam Virginal Book

(Ex.99 cont.)

Early examples of ground bass are found in some of the tutors published in the middle of the seventeenth century. Christopher Simpson in the *Division Violist* (1659) shows how the player was expected to improvise divisions (i.e. splitting long notes into smaller ones) whilst the keyboard player repeats the same phrase. This was extempore playing and was known as Divisions, or Divisions on a Ground, but there are many examples of written-out ground basses. The English composers of the seventeenth and eighteenth centuries wrote many ground basses. Examples abound in Purcell. There are several in *Dido and Aeneas*, the most famous being Dido's lament 'When I am laid in earth'. Other examples are 'Sound the Trumpet', the opening orchestral section of the anthem 'Rejoice in the Lord alway', and, on a large scale, act IV of *King Arthur*. Four or eight bars is the normal

length of phrase used for a ground bass, and since the bass ends
with a cadence, the whole divides into well-defined sections.
The bass phrase is announced by itself at the beginning and often
the upper parts become more complicated at each successive
appearance of the bass. One of the ways of obtaining variety
is for the melody to have different phrase lengths from the bass.
Purcell frequently does this. Dido's Lament is the supreme
example, but others occur in this opera and throughout the
anthems and cantatas. In scene three of 'Dido' the solo 'Oft she
visits this lone mountain' has a bass of four bars in continuous
quavers which appear with the voice seven times. The vocal
line has the following phrase lengths (in bars), 4, 4, 3, $2\frac{1}{2}$, $2\frac{1}{2}$,
$4\frac{1}{2}$, 2, $2\frac{1}{2}$, $3\frac{1}{2}$. This adds up to $28\frac{1}{2}$ (the extra half-bar making
the ending). So the voice has nine phrases with seven repetitions
of the bass, and squareness that is associated with ground basses
is absent. The very fact of an incessant ground bass, trying as
it were to fix the music in a rigid mould, creates musical tension
as the voice disregards it and triumphs against it. Another
feature of Purcell's ground basses is the way he shifts the key-
centre; this also avoids monotony.

Ex. 100 is a section of a ground by John Blow* for keyboard.
The four-bar ground appears 14 times and the extract shows

John Blow, Ground
bars 21–26

Ex. 100

* Contemporaries of Purcell ed. Fuller-Maitland (J. W. Chester.)

the sixth and part of the seventh. There is neat dovetailing in the quaver movement that ends the sixth variation and begins the seventh. (Ex. 100)

The early operatic composers used ground basses in their attempt to give their works unity and length. Practically the whole of scene 11 of Monteverdi's opera *L'Incoronazione di Poppaea* is built on ground bass. Variety is obtained by the insertion of short orchestral interludes (sinfonias).

The formula runs thus: sinfonia, solo over a ground bass by Ottone, sinfonia, solo over a ground bass by Poppaea. This is all twice repeated and the scene ends with a few bars of duet. The effect is not so stilted as it appears because although the bass is the same for the two characters the pitch is varied.

Other forms allied to the ground bass were the passacaglia and chaconne. These titles were used indiscriminately by composers to describe three types of composition: (a) a ground bass, (b) a continuous set of variations based on an harmonic progression, (c) a rondeau (chiefly used by French composers).

Examples of these three types with the title of passacaglia are (a) Bach's Passacaglia from *Passacaglia and Fugue in C minor* for organ (but occasionally the bass makes an excursion into the treble), (b) The last movement of Handel Suite VII, (c) Georg Muffat, *Passacaglia from Apparatus musico-organistus* (HAM 240).

Examples of these three types with the title of chaconne are (a) Buxtehude's *Chaconne* for organ, (b) Chaconne from Bach's Unaccompanied Sonata No. 3 in D minor for violin, (c) Couperin *La Favorite* (Chaconne-Rondeau).

It is impossible therefore to distinguish between the two words.

Bach's Chaconne is built on a four-bar phrase which comes 64 times. Both melody and harmony change. The former quite considerably as new rhythmic figures are introduced, but the latter preserves its cadence point and there is always the underlying feeling of the opening progression even when the harmony is intensified by chromaticism. One never ceases to wonder at the great invention of Bach in building such a massive work, ranging through the whole gamut of emotions from a simple four-bar phrase.

Type (c) is not much different from the ordinary rondeau. The main recurring theme is not altered at later appearances and while in some cases the episodes could be said to be based on the harmony of the theme, this is not always so. This, however, is its link with the chaconne.

Other words used in the seventeenth and eighteenth centuries to signify variation form are Double (French) and Partita (Italian).

Double is chiefly used to describe the repetition of a dance movement with embellishments. In Bach's English Suite No. 1 there is a courante 'avec deux Doubles'. In the first double the ornamentation is mainly in the right hand, in the second the left hand has almost continual quaver movement. In English Suite No. 6 a sarabande is followed by a double. The well-known Air in C minor from Matheson's fifth suite is followed by two variations called double 1 and double 2. There is no formal difference between his treatment of the theme and that of Handel's Air from Suite No. 5 (*Harmonious Blacksmith*), which he entitles 'Air con variazioni' except that the Handel has five variations.

In chapter ten, partita was explained as the Italian word for suite, but it also describes a set of variations. The title of HAM 192 is Partite Sopra l'aria Romanesca (variations on the Romanesca melody) by Frescobaldi. Bach is one of many organ composers of the seventeenth and eighteenth centuries who wrote partitas on chorale melodies.

The word 'variation' was used by eighteenth-century composers and two well-known examples are Bach's 'Goldberg' variations and Handel's so-called *Harmonious Blacksmith*. Handel's variations show the usual formula that many eighteenth-century players could have improvised. The harmony is not varied, the change is in the figures used. The melody is in simple binary form and moves mainly in quavers. Variation 1 ornaments the right hand in semiquavers. Variation 2 the same in the left hand. Variation 3 has triplet semiquavers in the right hand and Variation 4 the same in the left hand. Variation 5 has demisemiquavers in the right hand building to a climax where the left hand has its share.

The 'Goldberg Variations' is one of the monumental works of Bach and is a chaconne-passacaglia type. Written for a double manual harpsichord, the 30 variations are all self-contained, but related to the theme harmonically. Not that the harmonies remain the same, sometimes the same bass is used with different harmony; but throughout there is a feeling of harmonic unity binding the variations together. Every third variation is a canon; Variation 3 a canon at the unison, variation 6 a canon at the 2nd, variation 9 a canon at the 3rd, and so on until every interval has been treated. Among the variations is a French overture and a fughetta; there are many examples of coloratura slow movements, dance movements, and there is real virtuoso keyboard writing.

The variations of Mozart and Haydn carry on the idea of embellishment found in the double. Chief prominence is given to varied presentations of the melody. The phrase lengths of the theme and its underlying harmony are retained and variety comes in the use of different figures. The theme is always apparent like a familiar figure in a different dress.

Mozart's first variations were written when he was a boy and throughout his life he wrote many sets. From a study of them one finds certain features recurring. Apart from the usual ways of ornamenting a theme with quicker notes and using characteristic rhythmic figures, one generally finds one variation in the opposite mode, another at a much slower tempo and the last usually fast, often with a change of time-signature. The popular set that begins the pianoforte sonata in A (K.331) is described below. The theme is in $\frac{6}{8}$ time in two sections each ending with a double bar. The first is a complete sentence with an imperfect cadence at bar 4, answered at bar 8 with a perfect cadence. Bars 9–12 extend the opening phrase and end with a cadence in the dominant, bars 13–18 repeat 5–8 with a coda.

Variation 1. Same harmonic scheme with the theme embellished in semiquavers.

Variation 2. Same harmonic scheme using triplet semiquavers. The repeat is written out and further varied, so this variation looks twice as long as the theme.

Variation 3. In tonic minor, but the basic harmony is still recognisable although it is changed slightly. An expressive right hand melody with a simple accompaniment.

Variation 4. Back to A major with technical interest in the crossing of hands. A simplified quaver version of the theme, except for the opening of the second part which is more florid. Harmony as in theme.

Variation 5. A long melody of coloratura type at a slow tempo. Harmony as in theme.

Variation 6. Time changes to $\frac{4}{4}$ with the original harmonic scheme but at a fast tempo making a brilliant finish with an 8-bar coda.

The same plan is followed in the Sonata in D (K.284). The first six variations change the figures, variation 7 changes the mode, variation 8, 9, 10 restore the mode and exploit figures, variation 11 is a long slow one and variation 12 changes the time signature.

In the string quartet in D minor (K.421) the last movement is a theme and five variations—allegro in $\frac{6}{8}$ time. The first two variations keep close to the theme and so does No. 3 with its effective solo for viola. No. 4 is a beautiful major version and No. 5 keeps in $\frac{6}{8}$ but is marked 'piu allegro'. The second part of the theme is altered and extended to make the coda.

Haydn wrote sets that remain close to the theme and show the usual eighteenth-century method of ornamentation. The most well-known set is probably in the string quartet Op. 76 No. 3, variations, the Emperor's Hymn. He did not write many sets of this type, there is only one in the complete pianoforte sonatas (Sonata in A No. 30) but there are several in a form he evolved from C. P. E. Bach.* Examples are the slow movements of the symphony in E flat (*The Drum Roll*) and two of the symphonies in D (the *London* and the *Clock*). The structure is best described as a mixture of rondo and variations. A theme is presented and is followed by another in the opposite mode. The first is then varied and usually the second also. The first then may appear again further varied. The formula is ABABA which shows some

---

* Tovey. Article on Variations in *Encyclopaedia Brittannica*.

affinity to rondo form. Really to be in rondo form, the second appearance of B should be replaced by a new theme C. It is the juxtaposition of B in the opposite mode from A that gives this form its special character. Sections A and B are usually in two parts, each repeated, and sometimes in later appearances Haydn writes out the repeat with a further variation, or he may let the repetition of the first part remain undecorated and vary the repeat.

The slow movement of the Drum Roll symphony is set out below:

The Drum Roll. A (C minor), B (C major), A² varied, B² varied, A³ varied, B³ varied and developed and then first section of B repeated as a finale.

The following examples are from the pianoforte sonatas.

No. 22 in E (last movement)

A (E major), B (E minor), A² varied on repeat, B² varied, A³ varied on repeat.

No. 29 in F (last movement)

A (F major), B (F minor), A² varied, A³ varied on repeat.

No. 33 in D (last movement)

A (D major), B (D minor), A² varied, B² varied, A³ first part varied on repeat.

No. 34 in E minor (last movement)

A (E minor), B (E major), A² (varied in 2nd part), B² varied, A³ (first part varied on repeat, second part both times).

No. 40 in G (first movement)

A (G major), B (G minor), A² varied, B² varied, A³ varied.

No. 44 in G minor (last movement)

A (G minor), B (G major), A² (first part varied on repeat, second part varied but not repeated), B² not varied but shortened.

Several examples have been given because this form is not always easily recognised. There are other examples in the string quartets of Haydn. One of the best examples is the Variations in F minor for piano which is on a scale comparable to the slow movement of the *Drum Roll Symphony.* Haydn had an understanding of the variation principle and there are many movements not in variation form where he varies later appearances of the themes. The first movement of Sonata No. 48 in C major where the form described above is further intensified by the likeness of A to B is a movement well worth analysis.

Beethoven makes use of the Haydn form, although it never appears exactly as in Haydn. The slow movement of the 9th Symphony has variations on two melodies but they have not the simple major-minor relationship of Haydn. The form of this movement may be described as theme A in B flat, theme B in D major, A^2 varied in B flat, B^2 varied in G, A^3 varied in E flat and C flat, A^4 varied in B flat, coda.

This form also appears in the slow movement of the quartet in A minor Op. 132 and other varieties are the slow movements of the 5th and 7th symphonies.

There are several sets of variations by Beethoven which do not merit serious study as typical compositions such as those on *God save the King* and *Rule, Britannia*, but as Apel says* 'With Beethoven the variation form reached its all-time peak'. He gives each variation its own special character. Some idea is taken that develops in its own right and yet has links with the theme; some feature of the theme makes a starting-point and then the variation grows out of it. Yet generally it is worked out in the same phrase-lengths as the theme and gives the impression of moving along the same orbit as the theme. It is another example of the ideal of all composition, 'Unity in variety'. There must be a sufficient connection between variation and theme to make the relationship evident. The usual practice is for the first few variations to be simple by means of melodic decoration only. The reiteration of the harmony with its cadence point continues the impression made by the theme. With this preparation the listener will recognise later a variation which matches the theme in phrase-length, although its constituent parts may be changed.

As an example of Beethoven's method the variations from the pianoforte sonata in A flat Op. 26 will be analysed. Although this is a fairly early work it already shows the line of departure that Beethoven had taken from his predecessors.

* *Harvard Dictionary of Music.* Harvard 1944.

Andante con variazioni, Beethoven Op. 26 Key A flat in $\frac{3}{8}$ time

The theme is 34 bars long and consists of a phrase of 8 bars ending on the dominant with an answering phrase of 8 bars almost the same, ending on the tonic. Each of the 8-bar phrases divides into two of 4 bars. A short modulatory section of 10 bars that emphasises the dominant leads back to the tonic for a repetition of bars 9–16. AABA—the melody and harmony are simple with well-defined cadence points.

Variation 1

In the same mood as the theme and the harmony is unchanged, but the melody develops an arpeggio figure, except for the cadences, where the original melody shines through. The first phrases beginning in the lower register of the keyboard and gradually extend to the higher.

Variation 2

The theme is in the left hand, sometimes in the bass but more often in the tenor. A different mood is obtained by the continuous demisemiquaver movement, the left hand has mainly semiquavers and the right hand demisemiquavers off the beat.

This figure maintained all through throws a spotlight on the theme and the interest is more in the continual excitement of the figure than in any musical development.

Variation 3

A slow variation, intense and dark in the key of A flat minor. The harmonic scheme is kept (in a minor version) for the first three bars of the 'A' phrases, the ascending harmonies being continued with a syncopated melody that lags behind, causing strong discords that resolve relentlessly upwards bar after bar. The inexorability of the resolution has the force of some great natural phenomenon. The cadence at the 4th bar is bypassed, but the strong ones at bars 8 and 16 are kept and provide the link with the theme. The mood of the opening eight bars is intensified in the written-out repetition, with the ascending harmonies underlined by a sforzando bass note.

A variation of great power and character and yet all emanates obviously from the theme.

Variation 4

A scherzo of feathery lightness built on the original harmonic scheme with a few touches of chromatic colour. The tempo is faster and after the first few notes of the theme the whole jumps up an octave for the next few and then down again. The leaping effect continues and the dance becomes more excited as the leaps and consequent falls stretch almost to two octaves.

Variation 5

The harmonic scheme is preserved, the melody is ornamented first in semiquaver triplets and then later in demisemiquavers (bar 17). The mood of this last variation is shown by the word 'dolce' at its head. It is a sweet, full-sounding version. A coda of 15 bars brings what appears to be a new four-bar melody but which in its simplicity and mood seems to be the essence of the theme. The four bars are ornamented, and the last four notes are repeated twice in augmentation bringing the piece gradually to its end.

Other variations in Beethoven's early and middle periods are string quartet in A Op. 18 No. 5 (third movement), Septet Op. 20 (third movement), 32 variations in C minor, the Kreutzer Sonata for violin and piano Op. 47 (second movement), Variations on an original theme Op. 34 (the variations are in different keys), 15 variations with a fugue on a theme from Prometheus Op. 35 (*Eroica Variations*).

As Beethoven's genius developed, his variations became more individual. Each work is a separate entity and must be approached as such. Apel's 'all time peak' is best shown in the Diabelli variations Op. 120 which has been so admirably dealt with by Professor Tovey★ that other comment seems superfluous. Other sets of this period are to be found in the pianoforte sonatas Op. 111, Op. 109, string quartets Op. 127, 131, 135, the pianoforte trio Op. 97. The slow movement of the 9th symphony has

★ *Essays in Musical Analysis Vol. IV*. Oxford University Press.

been mentioned earlier in connection with the major-minor form of Haydn, but the choral variations in the last movement should be examined.

After Beethoven perhaps the greatest writer of variations is Brahms although Schubert, Schumann, Mendelssohn and Liszt all wrote in the form. Among Schubert's variations are the *Wanderer Fantasia*, those on *Death and the Maiden* in the string quartet in D minor, the variations in the Octet and the B flat major Impromptu for pianoforte. He puts forward no new structural ideas, but his variations are always coloured by his sense of drama which is strongly shown by his choice of chords and modulations. His ability as a melodist endows his themes with a memorable quality. Schumann's 'Etudes Symphoniques' are variations of the free kind in which the variations do not keep within the framework of the phrase-lengths of the theme and have at times only the slenderest of links with it. This aspect of variations will be more fully discussed later. Mendelssohn kept to the decorative principle in the variations in the Organ Sonata No. 6 and in the pianoforte variations also he is fairly strict. Liszt in the Rhapsodies and Paganini studies makes his variations real virtuoso piano writing but apart from this adds little new to the form.

Brahms can be said to have begun with the scheme as found in early and middle Beethoven. He wrote a large number, chief of which are those on a theme of Handel (Op. 24) and those on a theme of Paganini (Op. 35) for pianoforte. In his chamber music there are the variations in the clarinet quintet Op. 115, the string sextets in B flat (Op. 18) and G (Op. 36) and most famous of all, the St. Anthony Variations for orchestra. Brahms seems content with the classical restriction of matching the phrase-lengths of the variations with those of the theme, and like Beethoven he endows each variation with character, in spite of its nearness to the theme. But since he lived in a later age his classical leaning is tempered by the influence of romantic harmony. The rhythmical ingenuities that are a feature of his style show another difference from Beethoven.

A great deal of the aesthetic satisfaction in music (and in other works of art for that matter) comes from the triumph of spirit over matter. When Brahms in the 'St. Anthony' variations keeps so close structurally to the theme and yet gives each variation its individual character and emotion we cannot help applauding the mastery. These variations keep in the concert programmes because of their musical beauty, but to a student the musical beauty is enhanced by the technical triumphs. It is an interesting exercise to write in and play the melody, altering it to fit the various time-signatures of the different variations. Thus the horn melody of variation 3 and the syncopations of variation 5, the lilting $\frac{6}{8}$ melody of variation 7, and the dark thin writing of variation 8 are shown to be related to the theme. Three are written in Ex. 101.

The five-bar phrases add another distinctive element. The two sections of the theme are repeated, sometimes indicated by repeat marks, but often written out in full. In the latter case the repeat is slightly different and there is the additional effect of a repeat with variations. Brahms pays allegiance to the older tradition by a finale on a ground-bass constructed from the opening five bars, part theme and part bass. After 16 appearances the theme is sounded fortissimo in the treble, the mind having been prepared for it by appearances in diminution. Thus the wheel comes full circle; after all the experiences of variation the quiet devotional opening evolves as a triumphal conclusion. Brahms's essays in variation form include the great chaconne-passacaglia that ends the fourth symphony. This by its very strictness and self-imposed limits—the phrase structure is identical for 30 presentations of an eight-bar phrase—is impressive.

Elgar in the *Enigma Variations* kept fairly close to tradition regarding form, although the individuality of the people he is describing* causes him to make each variation really distinct.

In the main, however, composers after Brahms are more free. Strauss in *Don Quixote* wrote variations that are so free that they would have gone unrecognised in the classical period. The tendency after Brahms was to expand the method used in the 'Andante and Variations' and 'Etudes Symphoniques' of Schu-

* 'To my friends pictured within.'

Ex. 101

Brahms, 'St. Anthony' Variations, Op. 56a
Variation 3, bars 44–47

mann. He took a characteristic figure out of the theme, developed it and made a movement that stood alongside the theme in its own right. The classical adherence to the phrase length and harmony of the theme was abandoned and the connection between theme and variation was often very tenuous. Composers sometimes go back to the old methods, as Tchaikovsky did in the variations of the Pianoforte Trio in A minor, but this is the exception.

The older chaconne-passacaglia type has attracted later composers as, for instance, Britten in *Peter Grimes* and the second
string quartet. Variations are almost a necessity in ballet music
which has given a stimulus to the form. The near-passacaglia
in Bliss's *Miracle in the Gorbals*, and the sets of variations for the
seven deadly sins in Walton's *Quest* as well as the ground-bass
in a later scene are examples.

This chapter ends with a list of some of the ways in which
classical composers varied a theme. Although they are set out
singly, they are more often found in combination.

(1) Ornamenting the melodic line of the theme.

(2) Changing the note-lengths of the theme.

(3) Using a rhythmic figure in which the notes of the theme
     can be preserved.

(4) Colouring the harmony by use of chromaticism but
     keeping the main progressions and the cadences.

(5) Altering or completely changing the harmony.

(6) A new melody with the original harmony.

(7) Changing the register.

(8) Changing the mode.

(9) Changing the speed.

(10) Treating the theme contrapuntally.

(11) Using some portion of the theme or its rhythm as a basis
      for development.

CHAPTER FIFTEEN

Later Trends

The forms described in this book, and the illustrations chosen, are drawn mainly from the seventeenth century to the middle of the nineteenth century. What of the form of the music after this period? There seemed to be no need for new forms. Composers were seeking for new types of melody and were increasing the harmonic vocabulary, but this was done mainly within the framework of the existing forms. The grandiose ideas of the later Romantic and Nationalist composers needed more length in the movements and so the forms were expanded, but they were still recognisable as sonata form, rondo form, ternary form, etc. In the previous chapters of this book composers were mentioned by name and their works analysed. This was possible because of the thousands of composers only a comparative few have survived, and of those few one can quote those who made a contribution to musical form. In the recent past and present the names are still legion, and time has not completed its sifting process. We are all too close to them to be able to say who will stay the course. 'Because we have knighted the great Smith and play his works constantly, it does not follow that a note of his will be heard 200 years hence'.* This does not mean that it is impossible to analyse the works of all these composers but that each should have a chapter to himself. Such treatment is outside the scope of a book of this size, and even if it were done the overall picture would be unclear. It is possible to generalise about the forms used by the composers of the immediate past, but one must take into account the disadvantage that goes with any generalisation. One can say that in some of the symphonies by composers such as Sibelius, Mahler, Bruckner, Elgar, there are the normal four movements and the individual forms are still

* Adam Carse, *The Orchestra in the Eighteenth Century*, p. 5.

akin to those of classical times. It would seem natural that the composers who have still kept a link with the diatonic and chromatic harmony of the nineteenth century would also wish to keep to the forms used then. Even when this link through development over the years becomes very tenuous or indeed non-existent, there is still room for sonata form. Bartók, for instance, used sonata form for the first movement of all his concertos (except the first piano concerto). In his violin concerto the third movement is also in sonata form. The violin and viola concertos both end with a rondo.

The twelve-note system of Schönberg and his followers gave music a new language. Music was not built on a diatonic scale with chromatic additions, but on a chromatic scale in which every note was equal. Chords in the old sense had disappeared. There was no tonic because when every note is equal none can be foremost. The listener had to free his ear from classical sounds and listen in a completely new way, if that were possible. If he had followed Schönberg from his Wagnerian beginnings through his atonality to the tone-row he would have had some preparation for these new sounds. In a strict 12-note composition all the music is related to the original tone-row—a presentation of the 12 notes in the order chosen by the composer—and consists of inversions or transpositions of these 12 notes. In practice, however, although the tone-row begins by being the basis, it is often forgotten or used only in part, and the music reverts to atonality or even to diatonic harmony. The form of a 12-note piece tends to become self-contained. The repetition at different pitches and in different voices of the tone-row or its technical transformation give the whole coherence (at least from the visual aspect of the score), but it is undoubtedly difficult, if not impossible, to hear and grasp this complexity. In Schönberg's *Suite for Klavier* Op. 25, one of the earlier works on the 12-note system, when he was more strict at keeping to the tone-row than in his later works, the titles of the movements are still the familiar ones of Praeludium, Gavotte, Musette, Intermezzo, Menuett, and Gigue. Except for the Intermezzo they are common eighteenth century movements. The Menuett is in two sections and is followed by a trio, also in two sections. There is, therefore, an overall ternary structure when the Menuett follows the Trio and a binary structure for the Menuett and for the Trio. But there the resemblance to eighteenth-century method ends. The composition built on varied presentation of the tone-row has little in common with the balanced eighteenth-century phrases. The rhythmic figures give a unity and there is some use of sequence, but the inner life in the use of the tone-row is its chief cohesive factor. Alban Berg, one of Schönberg's pupils, seems to be able to make some compromise between the 12-note system and the diatonic. In the violin concerto the order of the tone-row encourages diatonic sounds and the composer is able to include without impropriety the Bach Chorale 'Es ist genug' and a folk melody. Without going into detail there is large-scale form in the construction of the four sections of the concerto and within each section the inherent unity due to the use of the tone-row. Stravinsky also in his latest compositions makes use of the tone-row. His life spans a long period (b. 1882) and a full-length book would be necessary to show his attitude to form. It would necessarily include his own definition of the word in 'Poetics of Music'. It is a long journey from the simple structures of *Firebird* (1910) to the sparse serialism of *Abraham and Isaac* (1963).

Since the war there have been many attempts to find new ways of writing music. Some are following or reverting to the 12-note path and are evolving their own style in this language. Another experiment that has been developed is 'Musique concrète'. The method is to record certain sounds, musical or non-musical, to alter them or to distort them mechanically and then to re-present them. The sounds may be altered by change of pitch or speed, or they may be played backwards. The distortion might be made through the addition or omission of harmonics. The final sound would be a 'mix' worked out by the composer. It is argued that the result must have some formal unity as there must be a relation between the original sounds and the altered or distorted ones. 'Musique concrète' has been superseded by electronic music in which sounds are built up synthetically. By this means it is possible to imitate any instrumental sound, but it is also possible to make sounds that are completely new. These new sounds necessitate new methods of composition, but as yet this method has not produced any memorable composition. An effective use of electronic music is in its conjunction with normal 'composed' music. The American composer Varèse in 'Déserts' interspersed recorded sections with instrumental ones. At a first hearing it is noticeable that the recorded sections are in sympathy with the emotional state of the music that precedes them and they dovetail into the instrumental returns. Further hearings familiarise one with the instrumental sections, but it is difficult to distinguish any plan about the electronic sounds. For these newer types of music we have not yet evolved a language that can be used for analysing the relationship of the sounds to one another, or the structure as a whole. By the time this has come about they will no longer be regarded as 'new' and the rising generation will be experimenting with yet more up-to-date idioms. This is the course of events so familiar to the historian. What is hailed as the 'new' music becomes accepted and is regarded as part of the established order by the next generation, who seek for further ways of enlarging the musical vocabulary.

Whatever course music follows there are essential requirements of design that must be present if music is to maintain its appeal to successive generations. The minimum requirements are first, there must be a feeling of unity about the whole, second, there must be contrast in the constituent parts, and, third, there must be logical development for the music to appeal to the mind as well as the heart.

APPENDIX ONE

Glossary Index

Where there is more than one reference, the most important one
is given first.

ABENDLIED (Ger.) Evening Song.

ABRIDGED SONATA FORM. Chapter Six, also p. 52.

ACCOMPANIED FUGUE. p. 131.

AIR (1) A song; (2) A movement of the eighteenth-century suite in which
the melody is important. Bach's Partitas Nos. 4 and 6 and French Suite
No. 4 contain Airs. pp. 85 and 87.

AIR WITH VARIATIONS. Chapter Fourteen, also pp. 52, 69, 79, 87.

ALBORADA (Sp.). A species of rustic instrumental music sometimes played on
bagpipes and drum, originally a morning song. Rimsky-Korsakov in
Capriccio Espagnole and Ravel in *Miroirs* have made use of it.

ALBUMBLATT (Ger.). Album leaf. A short simple piece that would be suitable
for an autograph album.

ALLEMANDA (It.), ALLEMANDE (Fr.). p. 88, Chapter Ten.

ANACRUSIS. p. 6.

ANGLAISE (Fr.). A rarely used dance of the eighteenth-century suite (see Bach
French Suite No. 3) in fairly fast duple time, p. 87. Also describes any
dance of English origin.

ANSWER. The second statement of the subject in a fugue (*q.v.*), p. 122, Chapter
Thirteen.

ANTECEDENT. The first voice in a canon, p. 110.

ANTHEM. A short choral composition to biblical or sacred words suitable for
a church service.

ARABESQUE (Fr.). A melodic counterpart of fanciful Arabian architectural
ornamentation. Schumann has used the title for characteristic pieces in
which the melody is ornamented.

ARIA (It. lit., Air). (1) A vocal solo with instrumental accompaniment. The
word generally refers to the numerous vocal solos of the seventeenth and
eighteenth centuries in which the first section is repeated after the second
(ABA). (See Aria Form *q.v.*). (2) An instrumental movement in which
the 'air' is important.

ARIA FORM. p. 22.

ARIETTA (It.), ARIETTE (Fr.). (1) A short aria generally without a middle section;
(2) The term is also applied to instrumental music of a similar nature.

ARIOSO (It.). A style rather than a form. (1) Vocal music that is something
between recitative and aria; (2) Occasionally (as in Beethoven Op. 110,
last movement) used of an instrumental piece in cantabile style.

ARSIN (Greek). Per arsin et thesin, pp. 108–9.

AUBADE (Fr.). Morning serenade of the type played in aristocratic circles in the seventeenth and eighteenth centuries. Used by nineteenth-century and later composers for short pieces of a light character.

AUGMENTATION. Lengthening a theme by doubling, trebling, quadrupling, etc. its note values, pp. 13, 108, 115, 127, 132, 133.

AYRE. A strophic English song of the sixteenth/seventeenth centuries accompanied by voices or instruments (generally the lute and bass viol).

BADINAGE, BADINERIE (Fr.). A light playful piece. Bach's Suite for flute and strings in B minor contains a movement entitled Badinerie.

BAGATELLE (Fr., Ger.). A short simple piece usually for pianoforte.

BALLAD. Originally a vocal accompaniment to a dance. Applied now to popular songs having the same music for each verse.

BALLADE (Fr.). A form of poetry and music sung by the trouvères. In eighteenth-century Germany the word was applied to poems of the Erlkönig type (*The Erl-King*, a poem by Goethe). When set to music they were usually 'durchkomponiert' (through-composed), i.e. the music for each verse is different. Pianoforte composers from Chopin onwards used the name for a work of a romantic nature. The form is generally free, but the Brahms Balladen are in ABA form.

BALLATA (It.). A fourteenth-century form of words and music highly organised. For details see HAM 51 and 53.

BALLETTO (It.), BALLET(T). (1) a vocal composition of about 1600 in dance style, usually with a fa-la refrain. An English example is Morley's 'Now is the month of maying!'; (2) An instrumental composition in similar style.

BARCAROLLE (Fr.). From Italian Barca, a boat. A lyric piece usually in $\frac{6}{8}$ or $\frac{12}{8}$ with an accompaniment illustrative of the quiet movement of water.

BASSO CONTINUO (It.). A bass part usually with figures below the notes indicating the harmony. Used mainly in seventeenth- and eighteenth-century music.

BASSO OSTINATO (It.). See Ground Bass, also p. 93.

BERCEUSE (Fr.). (1) A lullaby or cradle song; (2) A quiet instrumental piece with a prevalent rocking rhythm.

BINARY FORM. Chapter Three, also pp. 28, 29, 44, 53, 59, 66, 81, 86, 87, 93, 96, 98–103, 105, 135. COMPOUND BINARY. fn. p. 28.

BOGENFORM (Ger.). Forms having a structure similar to a 'bow' or an 'arch' (ABA: ABACABA).

BOLERO. A Spanish national dance of lively character, often accompanied by castanets. It is in $\frac{3}{4}$ time and uses rhythms such as $\frac{3}{4}$ ♫♫ ♫ or ♫♫ ♫ or ♫♫ ♫

BOURRÉE (Fr.). p. 90, also Chapter Ten.

BRANLE (Fr.). Brawl. A sixteenth century round dance of French origin generally in duple but sometimes in triple time. The dance had a swaying motion and was accompanied by singing.

BRIDGE PASSAGE. A connecting passage between two of greater importance. Generally used of the music between the first and second subject-group in sonata form, p. 34 and Chapters Five and Six.

BURLA, BURLESCO, BURLESCA (It.). Literally, a jest. A composition in this vein. Examples are in Bach's Partita No. 3 (p.86) and Schumann's *Albumblätter*.

CACCIA (It.). p. 110 and note on p. 111.

CADENCE. Chapter Two, also pp. 22, 35.

CADENZA. pp. 22, 68, 69, 79, 80.

CANCRIZANS. p. 108.

CANON. p. 107, also p. 103, Chapter Twelve and pp. 130 and 142.

CANONIC IMITATION. p. 111.

CANTATA. The word is used today to describe a short vocal piece, sacred or secular, for voices (solo or choral or both) with instrumental accompaniment. Cantatas were first written in the early seventeenth century and were in recitative style for a solo voice. Later, arias were added and A. Scarlatti wrote many consisting of two contrasting recitatives and arias. Secular cantatas were named Cantate da Camera in distinction to Church cantatas, Cantata da Chiesa. The word is familiar because of the Bach cantatas. In these the vocal forces range from a single voice to four soloists and chorus and there is orchestral accompaniment. The words are from the Bible or other sacred writings. A feature of many is the use of the music and words of the popular hymn-tunes (Chorales). They were performed before the sermon and were intended to further the Church's teaching. pp. 58, 130.

CANTILENA (It.). (1) A vocal piece, smooth and lyrical; (2) An instrumental piece in similar style.

CANTUS FIRMUS (L.). Literally fixed song, usually abbreviated to C.F. A melody forming the basis of a polyphonic composition. It was normally in the tenor in long notes, and the other voices wove their counterpoint in quicker notes around it. The C.F. might be a sacred or secular melody or merely a scale passage. p. 135.

CANZONA (It.). pp. 112, 113, 115, 121. Also in eighteenth and nineteenth century a name for a lyrical song or an instrumental piece of similar nature.

CANZONA FRANCESE (It.). 113.

CANZONET (It.). Diminutive of Canzona and used to describe (1) short vocal pieces of sixteenth and seventeenth centuries of a light style; (2) simple flowing songs of a later period, e.g. 'My Mother bids me bind my hair', by Haydn.

CANZONI DA SONARE (It.). p. 113.

CAPRICCIO (It.), CAPRICE (Fr.). The seventeenth-century form is described on p. 116 (see also p. 112), but the word was used by nineteenth-century composers for instrumental pieces of a capricious nature. (See also p. 86).

CASSATION. An eighteenth-century form of outdoor music generally with one instrument to a part. The form was allied to the Divertimento and Serenade. Normally there were more than four movements, some in symphonic form and others in dance form.

CATCH. p. 112.

CAVATINA (It.). A short solo song rather simpler than the aria. Applied also to instrumental music of a similar character.

CEBELL or CIBELL. A type of gavotte found in Purcell and his contemporaries. p. 85.

CHACONNE (Fr.). pp. 91, 140, 149, 151.

CHANSON (Fr.). The French word for song, and has had many meanings over the centuries. It generally refers nowadays either to (1) the polyphonic secular song of the sixteenth century or (2) a short song of a popular nature, common during the nineteenth century. In (1), the lines of the verses were often repeated and the work was split into short sections. The harmonic aspect became as important as the contrapuntal. p. 112.

CHANT. A term indicating the music of the church, especially in the early stages (Byzantine chant, Gregorian chant, etc.). In the Anglican and Protestant Churches, the music to which the psalms are sung: a single chant will fit one verse and a double chant two verses.

CHORALE. A hymn tune belonging to the German Protestant Church.

CHORALE PARTITA. Variations on a chorale (q.v.) usually for organ.

CHARAKTERSTÜCK (Ger., literally characteristic piece). An instrumental piece of a descriptive nature.

CHORALE PRELUDE. A composition based on a chorale, usually for organ.

CIACONA (It.). See Chaconne.

CODA (It., literally tail). A passage added to a movement to give a stronger sense of finality. pp. 28, 42, 68, 72, 129.

CODETTA (It.). A small coda. (1) In Sonata Form, a few bars rounding off the exposition (q.v.) of a movement, p. 35; (2) In Fugue, a short interlude which links one entry to another in the exposition, p. 124, also Chapter Thirteen.

COLORATURA (It.). Usually used to describe ornamental passages in vocal music; used also of sixteenth-century keyboard and lute music. The correct Italian word to describe this is FIORITURA.

COMES (L.). p. 110.

COMPOUND BINARY FORM. Name sometimes used for Sonata Form and which shows its origin in the word binary.

CONCERT OVERTURE. p. 83.

CONCERTANTE (Fr., literally of a concerto nature). p. 57. Is also used to describe the solo group in a concerto grosso. pp. 54, 61, 67.

CONCERTATO (It.). A name used in the eighteenth century for symphonies that had elements of a concerto nature; descendants of the concerto grosso, yet in the prevailing harmonic idiom. Haydn and Mozart both wrote such works.

CONCERTINO (It.). (1) The solo players in the concerto grosso (eighteenth century); (2) A smaller and lighter type of concerto (nineteenth and twentieth century).

CONCERTO (It.). Chapter Eight, also pp. 46, 54, 86.

CONCERTO GROSSO. Music for a group of soloists with orchestra, usually in three movements, composed in the seventeenth and eighteenth centuries. The soloists were called the Concertante or Concertino players, and the orchestra the Ripieno players. p. 61.

CONCERTSTÜCK (Ger., literally Concert piece). The name given by Weber and later composers to pieces similar to concertos but on a smaller scale and usually in one movement.

CONTINUO, see BASSO CONTINUO.

CONTRE-DANSE (Fr.). An English country dance.

CORANTO, CORRENTE (It.). p. 88, also Chapter Ten.

CORTÈGE (Fr., literally procession). Composition written in processional or march style usually of a solemn nature.

COUNTER-EXPOSITION. p. 126, also Chapter Thirteen.

COUNTER-SUBJECT. p. 125, also Chapter Thirteen.

COURANTE (Fr.). pp. 85, 88.

CSÁRDÁS. A Hungarian national dance. A sad slow section alternates with a quicker and wilder one.

CYCLIC FORM. pp. 55, 114.

DEVELOPMENT. p. 37.

DEVELOPMENT SECTION. p. 37, also Chapters Five and Six.

DIMINUTION. Shortening a theme by using notes a half or third, etc. of the original value. pp. 14, 108, 115, 127, 132, 133.

DIVERTIMENTO (It.). Allied to the Cassation (q.v.); a collection of movements which has elements of both suite and symphony, the former shown by dances and the latter by movements in sonata form. Usually written for strings or for small combination of both strings and wind or for wind alone.

DIVISION. (1) A set of variations written in the seventeenth and eighteenth centuries; so called because the long notes of the theme were divided into shorter notes in the variations, p. 138; (2) a long vocal run.

DOUBLE (Fr.). pp. 89, 141.

DOUBLE CONCERTO. A concerto for two instruments and orchestra.

DOUBLE COUNTERPOINT. Two melodic lines so constructed that each makes a satisfactory bass to the other.

DOUBLE EXPOSITION. pp. 68, 69.

DOUBLE FUGUE. p. 129.

DUMKA. A Slavonic folk piece which alternates often quickly between gaiety and sadness. Used by Dvořák. p. 79.

DUMP, DOMP. An early dance of a melancholy character. (Shakespeare in *Romeo and Juliet* mentions 'doleful dumps' and 'merry dumps').

DUX (L.). p. 110.

ECOSSAISE (Fr.). A country dance, possibly of Scottish origin (though it has nothing in common with the Reel or the Strathspey) popular in France and England *circa* 1800. Examples by Beethoven and Schubert are in quick $\frac{2}{4}$ time.

ELECTRONIC MUSIC. p. 154.

ELÉGIE (Fr.). A song or instrumental piece expressing lamentation.

ENTR'ACTE (Fr.). (1) An interval between the acts of an opera or play; (2) Music performed during the interval.

ENTRADA (Sp.), ENTRATA (It.), ENTRÉE (Fr.). An introduction or 'entry' piece.

ENUNCIATION. A synonym for 'exposition' in sonata form.

EPISODE. p. 128, also pp. 24, 25, 45, 48, 61, 70, 74, 83, 97, 116, 124, also Chapter Thirteen.

EPISODICAL FORM. pp. 22, 24.

EPISTLE SONATA. An instrumental piece played before the reading of the Epistle at Mass.

ESTAMPIE (Fr.). An instrumental form of the thirteenth/fourteenth centuries containing a number of sections which were repeated with a different ending. The sections were known as 'puncti' and the first ending 'ouvert' and the second 'clos'.

ETUDE (Fr.). A study.

EXPOSITION. The opening section of a composition where the main themes are presented for the first time. (1) In Sonata Form, from the beginning of the movement until the end of the second subject-group, see p. 32, also Chapters Five and Six and p. 83; (2) In a Fugue, from the beginning until all the voices have given out the subject or answer once. pp. 120, 98, also Chapter Thirteen. Some expositions include a Redundant Entry, that is, one of the voices gives the subject out for a second time. p. 124.

FANCY. The English for Fantasia (q.v.).

FANDANGO. A lively Spanish dance in $\frac{3}{4}$ time, usually accompanied by singing and castanets.

FANFARE. A flourish of trumpets.

FANTASIA (It.), FANTASIE (Fr. and Ger.). (1) A movement or group of movements in no set form, often suggestive of improvisation, p. 86; (2) A number of tunes taken from an opera and played consecutively; (3) Another name for Fancy (q.v.), pp. 115, 112, 121.

FARANDOLE (Fr.). A Provençal street dance usually in $\frac{6}{8}$ time accompanied by pipe and tabor.

FIGURE. p. 4.

FIGURED BASS. p. 92.

FINALE. (1) The last movement of a sonata or symphony or any composition in several movements; (2) The closing section of an opera.

FINAL SECTION. p. 129.

FIRST-MOVEMENT FORM. Another name for Sonata Form (q.v.).

FIRST SUBJECT. Chapters Five, Six and Seven.

FORLANA (It.), FORLANE (Fr.). A lively Italian dance in $\frac{6}{8}$ or $\frac{6}{4}$ time.

FREE FANTASIA. Another name for Development Section (q.v.) of a movement in Sonata Form.

FRENCH OUVERTURE. pp. 81, 88, 142.

FROTTOLA (It.). A simple type of Italian vocal music of the late fifteenth and early sixteenth centuries. The music was chordal with a melody in the top part and the sections were repeated.

FUGA PER CANONEN (L.). p. 107.

FUGAL ALLEGRO. pp. 81, 93, 99, 103, 129.

FUGATO (It.). p. 131, also 63.

FUGHETTA. pp. 131, 142.

FUGUE. Chapter Thirteen, also pp. 59, 87, 92, 98, 101, 103, 107, 113, 115.

FUGUE ON A CHORALE. p. 130.

FURIANT. A quick Bohemian dance in $\frac{3}{4}$ time but with changing accents. Much used by Dvořák. p. 79.

GALLIARD. An early Italian dance in quick triple time. It often followed the Pavan (q.v.). p. 84.

GALOP, GALOPADE (Fr.). A lively dance in duple time.

GAVOTTE (Fr.). p. 90, also Chapter Ten, p. 153.

GIGA (It.), GIGUE (Fr.). p. 90, also Chapter Ten and p. 153.

GLEE. An unaccompanied vocal composition usually for three or more solo male voices (including an alto). It is harmonic rather than contrapuntal and usually falls into a number of sections.

GOPAK. A lively Russian dance in duple time.

GROUND, GROUND BASS. A composition in which the opening bass phrase is repeated several times with different upper parts. pp. 137, 139, also 91, 92, 149.

HABANERA. A slow dance from Cuba in duple time having some affinity with the tango. Bizet has one in *Carmen* and Debussy and Ravel also used it.

HALLING. A vigorous Norwegian dance in duple time.

HORNPIPE. A lively English dance, originally in triple time, but later in duple time. In early days it was accompanied by an instrument of the same name. pp. 91, 67, also Chapter Ten.

HUMORESQUE (Fr.). HUMORESKE (G.). A title given by some nineteenth century composers to a piece of a good-humoured or capricious character. Generally short except for Schumann's Op. 20.

IMITATION. The repetition at a close distance by one part of a phrase that has previously occurred in another part. pp. 107, 127.

IMPROMPTU. A nineteenth-century Romantic piano piece. Although the title suggests an improvisatory style, the Impromptus of Schubert and Chopin have no special characteristics.

INFINITE CANON. p. 109.

INTERMEZZO. (1) Entertainment of a light nature between the acts of a more serious play or opera; (2) A musical passage inserted in an opera for some special purpose, i.e. in *Cavalleria Rusticana* (Mascagni) to suggest an interval of time between two scenes; (3) An instrumental piece of the nineteenth century sometimes of a lighter kind. (Schumann, Brahms.)

INTRADA (It.). An instrumental entrance piece often preceding a ballet.

INTRODUCTION. p. 33.

INVENTION. (1) A short contrapuntal piece; (2) A suite.

INVERSION. (1) Applied to music in at least two parts. A passage is said to be inverted when the two outside parts interchange; A melody is inverted when the intervals comprising it are sounded in the opposite direction, i.e. the rise of a 3rd becomes a fall of a 3rd, etc.; (3) A chord is inverted when one of its notes other than the root is in the lowest part. pp. 109, 116, 125, 127, 132, 133.

INVERTIBLE COUNTERPOINT. See Double Counterpoint.

ITALIAN OVERTURE. p. 81.

JIG. The English forerunner of the gigue (*q.v.*).

LÄNDLER (Ger.). A slow German dance in triple time.

LEITMOTIV (Ger.). A theme, usually short and striking, which stands for some character or idea. p. 55.

LESSON. The English word for suite, and often used in seventeenth and eighteenth centuries for a collection of pieces for keyboard. p. 84.

L'IDÉE FIXE (Fr.). p. 55.

LIED (Ger., literally song). (1) A song with German words; (2) It usually refers to the art song of the nineteenth century beginning with 'Gretchen am Spinnrade' by Schubert. Other notable composers of the German Lied were Schumann, Brahms, and Hugo Wolf.

LINK. A short passage of music usually joining two sections of a movement.

LOURE (Fr.). An old French dance, usually in $\frac{6}{4}$ time. p. 90, also p. 87.

MADRIGAL. A composition for unaccompanied voices, each part being individual both in melody and rhythm. Popular in England since Tudor times. The earlier fourteenth century Italian form was simpler.

MARCH. A composition in duple or quadruple time with a strongly marked rhythm. p. 85.

MARCHE FUNÈBRE (Fr.), MARCIA FUNEBRE (It.). A funeral march. p. 102.

MASQUE. A dramatic entertainment of music, singing and dancing, generally on a mythological subject. Popular in the sixteenth and seventeenth centuries.

MAZURKA. A Polish national dance in triple time. The phrases end on the second or the third beat, which is accented.

METAMORPHOSIS. The modification of a theme to give it a change of character. A device much used by Liszt but also by Berlioz, Wagner and other nineteenth-century composers. p. 79.

MIDDLE ENTRY. p. 127, also Chapter Thirteen.

MINUET. pp. 89, 67, 82, Chapter Ten, pp. 100, 101, 153.

MINUET AND TRIO. pp. 23, 52, 90, 154.

MINUET AND TWO TRIOS. p. 24.

MISSA (L.). The Mass.

MODE. The word refers either to (1) a scale or (2) rhythm. The most used notes in a composition, if placed in alphabetical order, form a scale. At different periods of musical history the scale varies because the order of tones and semitones is different. The word mode, qualified by a suitable adjective, describes this order. Thus major mode, T, T, ST, T, T, T, ST.; Dorian mode, T, ST, T, T, T, ST, T. In a narrower sense the word refers to the mediaeval church scales of which the commonest were the Dorian (as above), Phrygian ST, T, T, T, ST, T, T, Mixolydian T, T, ST, T, T, ST, T, and Aeolian T, ST, T, T, ST, T, T; (2) the six most used time-patterns in the thirteenth century were known as the rhythmic modes. They were all in triple time. The first was trochaic ♩♪ the second iambic ♪♩ the third dactylic ♩. | ♪♩ the fourth anapaestic ♪♩ | ♩. the fifth spondiac ♩. | ♩. the sixth tribrachic ♪♪♪

MODERN RONDO FORM. See Sonata-Rondo.

MODIFIED SONATA FORM. See Abridged Sonata Form. Chapter Six.

MORCEAU (Fr., literally a piece). A composition of no great importance.

MORISCA, MORESCA (Sp.). A Moorish dance in which the dancers disguised themselves by blackening their faces and wearing costumes. Possibly the origin of the English Morris dance.

MOTET. A sacred composition for chorus, usually unaccompanied.

MOTIV (Ger.), MOTIF (Fr.). A short musical idea.

MOTO PERPETUO (It.). A composition in which a flow of quick notes is maintained throughout. p. 97.

MUSETTE (Fr.). (1) A kind of bagpipe; (2) A pastoral piece with a drone bass. See Gavotte. p. 90, also pp. 67, 153.

MUSIQUE CONCRÈTE. p. 154.

MUTATION. p. 123.

NACHTMUSIK (Ger.). Literally night music. A composition of serenade character. See Cassation.

NOCTURNE (Fr.), NOTTURNO (It.). Originally a serenade; in more recent usage, a slow lyrical pianoforte piece of a romantic nature.

NONET. (1) Nine instruments; (2) A composition for nine instruments. p. 51.

NOVELETTE. A movement in variable form, romantic in character.

OCTET. (1) Eight instruments; (2) A composition for eight instruments.

OLD RONDO. Another term for Rondo Form distinguishing it from Modern Rondo or Sonata-Rondo. pp. 24, 45, 53, 61.

OPERA. A musical setting of a play, generally with solo voices, chorus and orchestra. Grand Opera has music throughout; but Light Opera (in German Singspiel and in French Opéra Comique) contains passages of spoken dialogue.

OPERA BUFFA (It.), OPÉRA BOUFFE (Fr.). Comic Opera.

OPERETTA. (1) A short opera; (2) A light theatrical entertainment with songs, dances and spoken dialogue.

ORATORIO. A musical setting of a sacred story usually for solo voices, chorus and orchestra.

ORDRE (Fr.). The French for Suite. p. 84.

OSTINATO (It.). See Basso Ostinato.

OVERLAPPING OF PHRASES. p. 10.

OVERTURE. An orchestral prelude to an opera, oratorio, or other vocal composition. An opening movement to a set of pieces. Operatic Overture p. 44. See Chapter Nine. Refer to entries in glossary under Concert Overture, French Overture, Italian Overture.

PARTITA. (1) A Suite (q.v.), p. 84; (2) A set of variations, p. 141.

PASSACAGLIA. p. 91, also pp. 87, 136, 140, 149, 151.

PASSAMEZZO (It.). A sixteenth-century dance in duple time, quicker than the pavan. Generally followed by a saltarello (q.v.).

PASSEPIED (Fr.). p. 90, also Chapter Ten.

PASTICCIO (It.). A work, usually an opera, which is made up by culling movements from other operas, or an opera which is the combined effort of several composers.

PASTORALE. (1) A cantata or stage work based on a rural subject; (2) A composition usually in $\frac{6}{8}$ or $^{12}_{8}$ time suggestive of the country.

PAVAN. A stately dance of Italian origin, in duple time. It often preceded the Galliard (q.v.), p. 84.

PEDAL POINT, POINT D'ORGUE (Fr.). A long held note normally in the lowest part whilst the upper parts have changing harmonies above it. The held note may also be in the top part (upper pedal) or in the middle (middle pedal).

PERIOD. p. 6.

PERPETUAL CANON. p. 109.

PERPETUUM MOBILE (L.). See Moto Perpetuo.

PHANTASIE, PHANTASIESTÜCK (Ger.). An imaginative piece of music. See Fantasie.

PHRASE. Chapter Two.

PIANO DUET. A composition for two players on one piano.

PIANO QUARTET. (1) Pianoforte, violin, viola and 'cello; (2) A composition for this combination.

PIANO TRIO. (1) Piano, violin and 'cello; (2) A composition for this combination.

POLACCA (It.). Polonaise.

POLKA. A Bohemian dance in $\frac{2}{4}$ time using the rhythm ♫ ♫♫ | ♫ ♪ ♩|

POLONAISE. p. 90.

POSTLUDE. An organ piece played at the end of a service.

POTPOURRI. A number of popular tunes played consecutively.

PRÉAMBULE (Fr.), p. 86. PREAMBULUM (L.). PRELUDIO (It.). PRELUDE. (1) The first of a pair or group of pieces, Chapter Ten; (2) The music at the beginning of a play or an opera or an act of an opera; (3) A piece complete in itself often of a romantic or descriptive nature.

QUARTET, QUATUOR (Fr.). (1) Four instruments or voices; (2) Music for four instruments or voices.

QUINTET. (1) Five instruments or voices; (2) Music for five instruments or voices. p. 52.

QUODLIBET (L.). A Potpourri (q.v.). Some of the tunes may be played simultaneously.

REAL ANSWER. p. 122 and Chapter Thirteen.

RECAPITULATION. p. 40 and Chapters Five and Six, also pp. 66, 68, 70.

RECITATIVE. Words set to music so that their natural emphasis is preserved. The melodic line is of secondary importance. When the recitative is accompanied by a keyboard instrument punctuating chords according to a figured bass it is known as 'recitativo secco'; when the accompaniment is written out fully and played by various instruments it is 'recitativo stromentato'. p.54.

RECTE ET RETRO (L.). See Retrograde motion.

RÉDUCTION (Fr.). An arrangement; generally applied to a 'piano reduction'; an arrangement for piano or a piece for instruments and/or voices.

REDUNDANT ENTRY. p. 126.

REEL. A quick dance in $\frac{4}{4}$ time, found in Scotland, Ireland and Northern England. Similar dances are found in Northern European countries. See Halling.

RÉJOUISSANCE (Fr.). A quick light orchestral piece of the eighteenth century, chiefly known through Bach's use in his Orchestral Suite, No. 4.

REPRISE. (1) Used today as a synonym for recapitulation; (2) Formerly used for the repeat of the exposition.

REQUIEM. A mass for the dead.

RESTATEMENT. Synonym for recapitulation or the repeat of the first section of a piece in ternary form.

RETROGRADE MOTION. A melody read backwards, i.e. from its last note to its first. p. 108.

RHAPSODY. A composition in the style of a Fantasia (q.v.) often founded on national airs.

RICERCAR, RICERCARE, RICERCATA (It.). pp. 112, 113, 115, 116.

RIDDLE CANON. p. 110.

RIGAUDON, RIGADOON. p. 91, also Chapter Ten.

RIPIENO. pp. 61, 63, 67.

RITORNELLO. (1) The repeated instrumental sections between the scenes of seventeenth-century operas (e.g. *Orfeo*, Monteverdi); (2) The instrumental prelude to a song, or the interludes between the verses; (3) A repeat, p. 23.

RITORNELLO FORM. Chapter Eight, also pp. 88, 98, 103.

ROMANCE (Fr.), ROMANZA (It.). (1) An instrumental piece in lyrical style; (2) In French, a sentimental song.

RONDEAU (Fr.). (1) A form used in mediaeval French music; (2) A form used in seventeenth-century instrumental music in which the opening melody was repeated with a 'couplet' in between each repetition, ABACADA, etc. p. 140.

RONDO FORM. Chapter Four and pp. 63, 69, 85, 88, 93, 100, 144, 153.

RONDO-SONATA. See Sonata-Rondo.

ROSALIA. A real harmonic and melodic sequence (*q.v.*) with the repetitions usually one degree higher.

ROTA. Mediaeval word for a Round (*q.v.*) generally applied to the Reading Rota (Sumer is i-cumen in).

ROUND. p. 112.

ROVESCIO (It.). Italian for retrograde motion.

SALTARELLO (It.). (1) A sixteenth-century dance in brisk triple time that followed a Passamezzo; (2) A quick Italian dance in $\frac{6}{8}$ or $\frac{12}{8}$ time.

SARABANDE. p. 89, also Chapter Ten, and pp. 95, 101.

SATZ (Ger.). Movement of a symphony or sonata.

SCENA (It.). A dramatic vocal composition with orchestral accompaniment.

SCHERZO. p. 52.

SCHOTTISCHE (Ger.). A round dance, not to be confused with the Ecossaise (*q.v.*). Rather like a slow Polka and known in England in the middle of the nineteenth century as the German Polka.

SECOND SUBJECT (THEME). p. 35, and Chapters Five and Six, also p. 68.

SEGUIDILLA (Sp.). A lively Spanish dance in triple time.

SENTENCE. p. 6.

SEPTET. (1) Seven instruments; (2) A composition for seven instruments.

SEQUENCE. The repetition, more or less exact, of a phrase at a higher or lower pitch. When a melody is repeated, the sequence is known as a Melodic Sequence. When the chords are repeated, the sequence is known as a Harmonic Sequence. The two types can be combined (see Rosalia). A Real Sequence is one in which the quality of each interval is exactly kept, so that each repetition is in a different key. If the quality of any of the intervals is changed, the sequence is Tonal.

SERENADE. (1) The music sung by a lover to his beloved; (2) See Cassation.

SERENATA (It.). (1) Italian for Serenade; (2) A cantata on a pastoral subject. Such subjects were popular in the eighteenth century.

SEXTET. (1) Six instruments or voices; (2) A composition for six instruments or voices.

SICILIANO (It.). pp. 91, 67.

SINFONIA (It.). Italian for Symphony (*q.v.*); (2) In seventeenth and eighteenth centuries, introductory pieces to an opera, church cantata or suite. pp. 86, 140; (3) Name used by Bach to describe his Three-part Inventions.

SINFONIETTA (It.). A small symphony.

SINGSPIEL (Ger.). Comic Opera with a spoken dialogue (i.e. *Il Seraglio*, Mozart).

SONATA. Chapter Seven, also pp. 57, 67.

SONATA À TRE (It.) See Trio-Sonata.

SONATA DA CAMERA (It.). pp. 84, 92, 95, 96.

SONATA DA CHIESA (It.). pp. 92, 95, 96, 113.

SONATA FORM (from about 1750 onwards). Chapter Five, also pp. 28, 83, 153, The Early Sonata, Chapter Eleven.

SONATA-RONDO. pp. 45, 27, 72, 79.

SONATINA. p. 56.

SONG FORM. p. 22.

SONG CYCLE. A group of songs of related thought and character designed to be sung consecutively and producing a musical entity. Well-known examples are Beethoven's Op. 98, An die ferne Geliebte (to the distant beloved) and Schubert's Die schöne Müllerin (the fair maid of the mill).

STRATHSPEY. A Scottish dance in $\frac{4}{4}$ time using the rhythmical feature known as the 'Scotch Snap' (♫).

STRETTO (It.). p. 127, also Chapter Thirteen.

STRETTO MAESTRALE (It.). p. 128.

STRING QUARTET. (1) Four stringed instruments: two violins, viola and 'cello; (2) Music for this combination (see Sonata). pp. 28, 51.

STRING TRIO. (1) Three stringed instruments usually violin, viola and 'cello; (2) Music for this combination.

SUBJECT (Fugue). Chapter Thirteen. See FIRST SUBJECT, SECOND SUBJECT.

SUITE. Chapter Ten, also p. 66.

SYMPHONIC POEM. A large-scale composition for orchestra based on a story or a 'programme' indicated by the title. p. 56.

SYMPHONY. Chapter Seven, also pp. 23, 28, 56, 57, 81, 83, 111, 131, 152.

TAMBOURIN (Fr.). An old French dance in duple time which takes its name from the Tambour (Eng. tabor) which accompanies it together with the pipe.

TARANTELLA (It.). A quick Italian dance in $\frac{6}{8}$ time, mainly in quaver movement.

TEDESCA (It. for the word 'German', i.e. a German dance). Alla Tedesca in seventeenth century meant in the style of an allemande. In the nineteenth century, the style of a Ländler (*q.v.*).

TERNARY FORM. Chapters Three and Four, pp. 29, 44, 52, 69, 88–90, 93. 98–103, 105, 129, 135, 154. Developed Ternary, p. fn. 28.

TERZETT (Ger.), TERZETTO (It.). A composition for three voices or three instruments.

THEME. A melodic subject (*q.v.*). For Theme and Variations see Air with Variations. Chapter Fourteen.

TOCCATA (It.). pp. 117, 86.

TONAL ANSWER. pp. 122, 123.

TONE POEM. See Symphonic Poem.

TRANSITION. (1) A section of music leading from one theme to another (see

Bridge-Passage); (2) An abrupt change of key.

TREPAK. A popular Russian dance in $\frac{2}{4}$ time.

TRIO. (1) Three performers, vocal or instrumental; (2) Music written for such a combination. p. 51; (3) The second section of a piece in Ternary form. See Minuet and Trio.

TRIO-SONATA. Compositions of the seventeenth and eighteenth century written generally for two violins and a bass ('cello or viol da gamba) and a keyboard instrument, usually a harpsichord to realise the figured bass. See Chapter Eleven where some trio-sonatas are analysed.

TRIPLE COUNTERPOINT. p. 53.

TRIPLE FUGUE. p. 130.

TUTTI (It.). pp. 67–70.

TWELVE-NOTE MUSIC. p. 153, 154.

VALSE (Fr.), WALZER (Ger.). A graceful dance of German origin in $\frac{3}{4}$ time.

VARIATIONS. See Air with Variations. Chapter Fourteen.

VORSPIEL (Ger.). p. 83.

VOX ANTECEDENS (L.). p. 110.

VOX CONSEQUENS (L.). p. 110.

APPENDIX TWO

Index of Music Examples

Haydn	Ex. 31–35	Sonata 48 in C major.
	Ex. 36	Symphony No. 7 in C major (Le Midi).
	Ex. 13	Sonata No. 38 in E flat major.
	Ex. 24	Quartet Op. 3 No. 6.
	Ex. 11	Symphony No. 88 in G major.
Mozart	Ex. 2	Sonata in C minor K.457.
	Ex. 17	Requiem. K.626
	Ex. 44–57	Piano Concerto in B flat K.450.
Purcell	Ex. 5	'Dido and Aeneas', Sailor's Song.
	Ex. 21	Trumpet Tune from 'Dioclesian'.
	Ex. 86	'Gloria Patri'.
	Ex. 87	'Allelujah'.
Rameau	Ex. 25	'Les Tendres Plaintes', Rondeau.
Schubert	Ex. 6	Octet in F major, Op. 166.
	Ex. 18	Sonata in A, Op. 120.
Schumann	Ex. 23	Little Folksong No. 9 from Album for the Young, Op. 68.
Torelli	Ex. 37–40	Concerto Grosso, Op. 8 No. 8.
Tye	Ex. 91	Anthem, 'Praise the Lord, ye children'.
Vitali	Ex. 72	Sonata for 2 violins and continuo.
Wagner	Ex. 4	'Flying Dutchman' Overture.

Miscellaneous

Hymn Tune	Ex. 20	'O God, our help', *St. Anne* (Croft).
	Ex. 8	'Praise to the Lord'.
Folk Song	Ex. 19	'The Holly and the Ivy'.
Old English Melody	Ex. 98	'Walsingham'.

APPENDIX THREE

Index of Composers and Compositions
(In addition to music examples listed in Appendix Two)

Index of References to the *Historical Anthology of Music*